十二天突破英语系列丛书

英汉翻译教程新说

武 峰 编著

内 容 简 介

本书将《英汉翻译教程》中三十篇文章的所有句子的翻译和《十二天突破英汉翻译》中的方法和技巧联系起来,将其中的一千多个句子进行了深入浅出的分析。本书可以认为是《十二天突破英汉翻译》的续集,是将前者的方法和技巧进一步付诸于实践,理论与实践并重,结果与过程并存,使读者都能读懂每个句子,了解翻译的过程,并将这些翻译的方法和技巧运用在自己的实践中。

图书在版编目(CIP)数据

英汉翻译教程新说/武峰编著. —北京:北京大学出版社,2013.5
(十二天突破英语系列丛书)
ISBN 978-7-301-22133-4

Ⅰ.①英…　Ⅱ.①武…　Ⅲ.①英语—翻译—高等学校—教材　Ⅳ.①H315.9

中国版本图书馆 CIP 数据核字(2013)第 026306 号

书　　　　名:英汉翻译教程新说
著作责任者:武　峰　编著
策　划　编　辑:吴坤娟
责　任　编　辑:吴坤娟
标　准　书　号:ISBN 978-7-301-22133-4/H·3247
出　版　发　行:北京大学出版社
地　　　　址:北京市海淀区成府路 205 号　100871
网　　　　址:http://www.pup.cn　新浪官方微博:@北京大学出版社
电　子　信　箱:zyjy@pup.cn
电　　　　话:邮购部 010-62752015　发行部 010-62750672　编辑部 010-62756923
　　　　　　　出版部 010-62754962
印　刷　者:北京市科星印刷有限责任公司
经　销　者:新华书店
　　　　　　787 毫米×980 毫米　16 开本　14 印张　329 千字
　　　　　　2013 年 5 月第 1 版　2022 年 12 月第 10 次印刷
定　　　价:45.00 元

未经许可,不得以任何方式复制或抄袭本书之部分或全部内容。
版权所有,侵权必究
举报电话:010-62752024　电子信箱:fd@pup.pku.edu.cn

为什么在翻译学习中译例这么重要?

——我的自序

这是十二天突破英语系列丛书的第三本,在前两本书中,我分别谈到了基础语法和基础翻译,特别是笔译。语法是翻译的基础,而且是笔译的重要基础。在《十二天突破英汉翻译》一书出版之后,我收到了很多反馈,大多数同学的主要问题在于,方法和技巧都可以看懂,但是苦于没有实践。我想这个问题有两个方面的解释。

第一,翻译是一门实践学科,特别是对于考翻译专业的研究生来说更是这样,所以,在我自己的翻译教学中一直秉承用译例说话的原则,方法和技巧向来都是实践的总结。任何不认识的单词,或是以方法至上的翻译教学活动都是不正常的,也是不可信的。从中国大学翻译的教学模式来看,教师一般都会选取一本经典教材,特别是把文章的翻译作为教学的主要内容。但是,同学往往听这些文章的翻译时都是昏昏欲睡,没有任何兴趣。问题在哪里?其实,问题就在于只有材料的堆砌,而没有方法和技巧的升华,更没有翻译过程的展现,也就是只有结果,而不注重过程。只有实践的实践没有任何意义,但是只有方法没有实践也是徒劳,所以,凡是一切想要走捷径的方法也都是注定失败的。学好翻译,只有将理论与实践相结合才是正道。

第二,《十二天突破英汉翻译》的最大弊端就在于,重理论而轻实践。出版之后,销量不错,但是,我心中一直惴惴不安,原因是只有理论存在，看起来过瘾，用起来难受，不免要遭到骂声一片。不过还好，中国近些年的英语教学大多是快餐式的，只要看起来过瘾就好，至于能不能出效果那就另当别论了。所以，在酝酿了很久之后，我决定用自己的方法和技巧来实践一些经典文章和段落，以此来弥补《十二天突破英汉翻译》的不足。实话实说，想要选取经典翻译材料来印证我的翻译方法和技巧就要选取一本好书。在茫茫书海中，我想到了庄绎传教授的《英汉翻译教程》。我在北外读研究生时就有幸得见庄绎传教授，并聆听了他的教诲，后来自己成为了翻译教师，也一直都用庄老师的书作为教材为本科生讲解翻译。庄老师也认为，翻译的实践——在笔译（也就是译例）中——是决定学习翻译成败的重要标志。所以，从我当翻译老师的那天起，就一直把译例当做重要的教学内容，在实践中收到了很好的效果。

再谈谈《英汉翻译教程》这本书吧，庄绎传教授在《简明英汉翻译教程》的基础上进行了修改，将原书中的一些文章进行了调整，最后定为十个单元，每个单元三篇课文，两篇英译汉，一篇汉译英，都有双语对照，其中第六单元和第七单元是文学，其余是非文学。这本书涵盖了政治、经济、文化、教育、地理等方面的文章，可谓是知识面广，涉及的文章体裁和题材也十分之多，可以堪称为经典教材。但是，书中也不乏一些问题，最突出的问题就是书中的译文和原文没有翻译过程的解释和展现，这也是大多数翻译书籍的弊端，重结果而轻过程，学生常常是一头雾水。所以，展现翻译过程成为现当代翻译教学的重要任务。

基于以上强调的译例的重要性和《英汉翻译教程》的经典性，所以我在2011年3月起在新浪微博上开设了"武哥教翻译"的栏目，将《英汉翻译教程》中三十篇文章的所有句子的翻译和我在《十二天突破英汉翻译》中的方法和技巧联系起来，用了近十五个月的时间，才将这本书的一千多个句子进行了深入浅出的分析，也受到很多学生的好评。后来，很多同学反映需要看到这本书的完整版，或是再把句子进行重新细致解构，所以，我才萌发了把这些材料整理出来进行出版的想法。

在后期的工作中，我把《英汉翻译教程》中的句子又进行了一些建设性的修改，对其翻译过程进行了解释，并把《十二天突破英汉翻译》的方法和技巧运用其中，最后定名为《英汉翻译教程新说》，将其归在了十二天突破英语系列丛书中。实际上，这本书可以认为是《十二天突破英汉翻译》的续集，是将前者的方法和技巧进一步付诸于实践。有的时候我认为这本书更加重要，因为它才是理论与实践并重，结果与过程并存。

我的想法很简单，就是希望所有阅读这本书的读者都能读懂每个句子，了解翻译的过程，并将这些翻译的方法和技巧运用在自己的实践中。在书中，我也预留了笔记区，就是让读者能把书中的生词或是短语记录下来以备不时之需。在书的开篇我也把所有翻译方法与技巧做出了总结，不至于让那些没有看过《十二天突破英汉翻译》的读者摸不着头脑。

一本拙著引来千言万语，最后还是说几句肺腑之言。在本书即将出版之际得知庄绎传教授由于年事已高而卧病在床，出版本书以对《英汉翻译教程》补充说明，也算是对老教授的一些慰藉吧。

在此，要感谢自己，十五个月以来的坚持，将一千多句子全部完成，并且不辞辛劳地进行校对和修改。

也要感谢孙丽娟女士在生活上和工作中所给予的无私关怀和支持。

也要感谢我的妈妈对我的养育之恩。

更要感谢北京大学出版社的吴坤娟编辑及领导和同事在图书出版过程中所给予的帮助和支持。

最后，我也要感谢这些年来帮助过我的同学、同事、亲戚、朋友和学生等，若没有这些帮助，我也定不能有今天任何一点小小的成绩。

当然，本书因出版仓促，难免有疏漏之处，若有不尽如人意之处，恳请读者提出批评，我一定加以改正。谢谢！

如有需要联系我的读者，请加我的新浪微博，网名是Brotherfive，电子邮箱是wufeng@bfsu.edu.cn。

武　峰

2012年国庆于北京外国语大学

Contents

翻译方法概述 ·· 1

Unit 1   Stories ·· 5

Unit 2   History ·· 21

Unit 3   Geography ··· 41

Unit 4   Economy ··· 61

Unit 5   Culture ·· 86

Unit 6   Literature (1) ··· 109

Unit 7   Literature (2) ··· 126

Unit 8   Popular Science ·· 147

Unit 9   Law ·· 167

Unit 10   Speeches ··· 189

翻译方法概述

翻译一直都是一门理论与实践相结合的学科，特别强调实践。本书的主要用途就是要将《十二天突破英汉翻译（笔译篇）》的基本方法运用到实践当中，所以在这里先将前一本书中提到的所有方法进行总结，这样可以让同学们更好地和更加清楚地记住这些要点，以便在使用本书的过程中能够随时查阅所讲到的方法和技巧。

1. 英译汉的主要步骤：第一步断句，第二步翻译，第三步重读译文。

2. 汉译英的主要步骤：第一步断句，第二步找谓语，第三步翻译，第四步重读译文。

3. 英译汉时，我们所遇到的句子类型有四种，如下表所示：

句子类型

种 类	解 决 方 法
长句，无逗号或是很少逗号。	先断句，再翻译，再重读。
长句，有大量逗号，无须断句。	先判断句与句之间的逻辑关系，再决定哪个先翻译，哪个后翻译，再重读。
长句，有大量逗号，有大量生词。	直接按照原有顺序翻译，查明每个生词的用法，最后重读让句子更加通顺。
短句，无逗号。	再短的句子也要有逗号，"剥洋葱"的翻译方法。

4. 中英文的三大差异。

中文善于用短句,且用逗号隔开;英文善于用长句,不用标点。

中文善于用动词,属于动态性语言;英文善于用名词,属于静态性语言。

中文是意合语言,所以句与句之间的连词比较少;英文是形合语言,所以句与句之间的连词较多。

5. 英汉互译中的四大规律。

第一,动词的过渡。在英译汉时,我们要用强势动词代替弱势动词;而在汉译英时,我们常用弱势动词代替强势动词。

第二,抽象名词的翻译。我们一般会认为在介词之前和冠词之后的名词是抽象名词,这是一种比较特殊的名词。在翻译的时候,我们有两种方法,一是如果这个名词有动词词根,我们就翻译为动词;二是如果这个名词没有动词词根,我们就增一个动词。

第三,增词与减词。从英译汉的角度来说,有四种增词的方法。一是增评论性词,常常出现在文学作品当中;二是增对象词和范围词;三是增范畴词;四是增动词。增动词又可以分为两种,一种是宾语前缺少动词,所以增动词,称之为"自然增词法";另一种是抽象名词的增词,称之为"人为增词法"。

第四,谓语动词的层次性。这个规律是专门阐述汉译英的,因为中文是动态性语言,所以动词较多。我们在汉译英时需要在很多动词当中找到哪个动词是主要的,而哪个动词是次要的。我们把最主要的动词作为核心谓语,把次要的动词作为非谓语动词或是从句,再次的动词作为介词,最不重要的动词不翻译。当然,我们在判断这些动词哪一个更重要的时候比较困难,因为这要判断句子之间和词与词之间的逻辑关系。

6. 八种译法。

在《十二天突破英汉翻译》中共提到八个要点的翻译,这对初学翻译的同学来说也是最重要的。所以在这里和同学们再来回顾一下。

第一，定语从句的翻译。定语从句按照"短前长后"的原则进行翻译，一般来说有三种译法，即前置译法、后置译法和句首译法。此外，在讲解定语从句的过程中，我们还说到了有关"循环套用"和"并列套用"的两种特殊情况。

第二，非谓语动词的翻译。非谓语动词如果在一个句子的最前面，那么我们首先要做的事情就是找主语；而非谓语动词如果在一个名词的后面，那么我们就认为这是一个定语从句，可按照定语从句的方法进行翻译。

第三，被动语态的翻译。中文里不善于用"被"字，而在英文中"被"却很常见，所以在翻译中我们主张用四种方法来避免"被"字在中文里出现。第一种，"被动语态变成主动语态"，这常见于没有宾语的被动语态；第二种，找"被"字的替代词，一般来说我们可以用"受到"、"遭到"、"为……所"结构等；第三种，在科技文献当中，我们用"可以"这两个字来代替"被"字；第四种，"有被不用被"的译法。

第四，英文中代词的译法。中文善于用名词或是省略，英文善于用代词，所以英译汉时要注意代词的译法。一般来说，我们翻译代词时有两点：第一点，代词指明要点；第二点，不抽象，不具体。

第五，英文中形容词和副词的译法。英文中的形容词和副词是两个比较活跃的词类，所以在翻译时我们要格外注意。一般来说，形容词和副词的翻译有三种方法。第一种，形容词和副词多用其延伸含义，一般不用其原意；第二种，形容词和副词可以互换，因为它们本身就是同源词；第三种，长的形容词和副词可以翻译成为一个短句。

第六，换主语的问题。中文是非平衡性语言，所以语句中各个部分长度不一,但是英语是平衡性语言,句子中的各个部分较平均。所以在翻译中,我们常常用换主语的方法来处理汉译英的问题。一般来说,汉译英换主语时主要有三种情况:第一种,偏正短语取"偏"做主语,然后想办法处理"正";第二种,在中文句子中找到"隐藏主语";第三种,无主语的句子我们可以用被动语态的方法来翻译,特别提到了"就近原则"。

第七,中文四字短语的翻译。中文里有较多的四字短语,所以我们在翻译的时候要格外仔细,一般来说有三种类型:一是AABB型,只翻译AB;二是ABAB型,只翻译AB;三是ABCD型,需要解释。

第八,"中国特色"词汇的译法。每个民族的语言中都有很多带有本民族色彩的词汇,中文也不例外,所以我们在翻译这些词语的时候既要尊重本民族的语言,也要符合英文的要求。一般来说,我们有三种译法。第一,直译法,用拼音直接写出这个单词,或是用英文直接翻译;第二,用增词的方法来进行解释;第三,在页面的底部用注释的方法解释句子中不容易理解的部分。

以上这些内容就是《十二天突破英汉翻译》的精华,当然除此以外我们还说到了很多其他的知识点,比如说中英文事实与评论的关系、"重译法"、直译与意译和有灵主语句与无灵主语句等。这些知识同样也是十分重要的,希望同学们能认真地实践这些要点。

Stories

Unit 1

The Quest 探索

本文的作者是艾格尼丝·史沫特莱，美国著名记者、作家和社会活动家，一位杰出的、与众不同的女性。1918年因声援印度独立运动而被捕入狱6个月。1919年起侨居柏林8年，积极投身印度民族解放运动，曾在柏林会见尼赫鲁。史沫特莱1928年年底来华，在中国一待就是12年。抗战初、中期，她目睹日本对中国侵略，向世界发出了正义的声音。本文摘自于她记述朱德生平《伟大的道路》一书，由梅念翻译。本文属于典型的非文学翻译，翻译方法体现得较多。

Taking the train, the two friends arrived in Berlin in late October 1922, and went directly to the address of Chou En-lai.

两个朋友乘坐火车，于1922年十月末到达柏林，并直接去往周恩来的住处。

注意 分词位于句首，先找主语翻译；时间和地点状语同时存在，先翻译时间再翻译地点；Chou En-lai是威妥玛式标音法。

Would this man receive them as fellow countrymen, or would he treat them with cold suspicion and question them cautiously about their past careers as militarists?

这个人会不会像同胞手足一样接待他们呢？会不会疑虑重重，详细询问他们军阀时代的经历呢？

注意 or连接的两个句子之间应当断句，用问号连接；这里的them可以直接翻译为"他们"，因为上一句话有指代；suspicion可以理解为抽象名词的译法，翻译为动词"疑虑"。

Chu Teh remembered his age.
朱德想起了自己的年纪。

注意 威妥玛式标音法；his这个单词是物主代词，第二次出现可以不翻译，在这里处理为"自己的"。

He was thirty-six, his youth had passed like a screaming eagle, leaving him old and disillusioned.

他三十六岁了，青春像一路鸣叫的鹰，早已一闪而逝，留给他的是衰老和幻灭。

注意 句子中的明喻，翻译时也要成为明喻；"一闪而逝"可以理解为评论，所以放在后面翻译。

When Chou En-lai's door opened, they saw a slender man of more than average height with gleaming eyes and a face so striking that it bordered on the beautiful.

周恩来的房门打开时，他们看见了一个身材消瘦、比普通人略高一点的人，两眼炯炯有神，面貌很引人注意，称得上清秀。

注意 slender在修饰男人时翻译要得体；这句话特别要注意的是偏正短语gleaming eyes翻译为主谓结构eyes are gleaming；border on the beautiful可以翻译为"清秀"，一般指男人。

Yet it was a manly face, serious and intelligent, and Chu judged him to be in his middle twenties.

而那是一张男子汉的脸庞，严肃而聪颖，朱德看他大概二十五六岁。

注意 yet的转折含义十分微弱，可以翻译为"而"；one's middle twenties可以理解为"二十岁的中间一部分"，所以翻译为"二十五六岁"。

Chou was a quiet and thoughtful man, even a little shy as he welcomed his visitors, urged them to be seated and to tell how he could help him.

周恩来举止优雅，待人体贴，招呼他们坐下，在询问他们有何见教的时候，甚至还有些腼腆。

注意 第一个从句中有同指现象，还有两个形容词的翻译；as在这里是表示时间状语，后面的he和him要指代具体，这里翻译为"他们有何见教"。

Ignoring the chair offered him, Chu Teh stood squarely before this youth more than ten years his junior and in a level voice told him who he was, what he had done in the past, how he had fled from Yunnan, talked with Sun Yat-sen, been repulsed by Chen Tu-hsiu in Shanghai, and had come to Europe to find a new way of life for himself and a new revolutionary road for China.

朱德顾不得拉过来的椅子，端端正正地站在这个比他年轻十多岁的青年人面前，用平稳的语调，说明自己的身份和经历：他怎样逃出云南，怎样会见孙中山，怎样在上海遭到陈独秀的拒绝，怎样为了寻找自己新的生活方式和中国革命的新道路而来到欧洲。

> **注意** 这是一个长难句，句首的现在分词和过去分词的用法要注意翻译；后面句中的who he was和what he had in the past分别处理为"身份"和"经历"；been repulsed被动语态的译法用"遭到"；而且本句中的时态处理十分得当，要注意体现一般过去时和过去完成时态。

He wanted to join the Chinese Communist Party group in Berlin, he would study and work hard, he would do anything he was asked to do but return to his old life, which had turned to ashes beneath his feet.

他要求加入中国共产党在柏林的党组织，他一定会努力学习和工作，只要不再回到旧的生活中，派他做什么工作都行，这种生活已经在脚下化为尘埃了。

> **注意** but翻译为"只要不"；被动语态如何处理；还有非限定性定语从句的译法，关系词which翻译为"这种生活"。

As he talked Chou En-lai stood facing him, his head a little to one side as was his habit, listening intently until the story was told and then questioning him.

他在说的时候，周恩来就站在他的面前，习惯地侧着头，一直听到朱德把话说完，才提出问题。

> **注意** as引导时间状语从句；后面as was his habit作为定语从句修饰his head，在这里处理为状语"习惯地"，某些情况下定语和状语可以互换，这是此句翻译中的难点；was told变被动为主动；him可以不翻译，直接将句子翻译为"提出问题"。

When both visitors had told their stories, Chou smiled a little, said he would help them find rooms, and arranged for them to join the Berlin Communist group as candidates until their application had been sent to China and an answer received.

　　两位来客把经历说完之后，周恩来一边微笑着，一边说他可以帮助他们找到住的地方，替他们办理加入党在柏林支部的手续，在入党申请书寄往中国而尚未批准之前，暂作候补党员。

> **注意** when可以表示"之前"、"之后"或是"同时"；arranged for意译为"替某人做某事"；as是"作为"；最后被动语态their application had been sent to China and an answer received使用了"有被不用被"的方法。

When the reply came a few months later they were enrolled as full member, but Chu's membership was kept a secret from outsiders.

　　过了几个月，回信来了，他们都成为正式党员，但是，朱德的党籍对外保密。

> **注意** 时间状语句首翻译；full member是"正式党员"，特别注意形容词full的译法；两个被动语态都是"有被不用被"的译法。

The Story of My Life 我的生活

本文的作者是海伦·凯勒，19世纪美国盲聋女作家、教育家、慈善家、社会活动家。她以自强不息的顽强毅力，在安妮·莎莉文老师的帮助下，掌握了英、法、德等五国语言。她完成了一系列著作，并致力于为残疾人造福，建立慈善机构，被美国《时代周刊》评为美国十大英雄偶像，荣获"总统自由勋章"等奖项。其主要著作有《假如给我三天光明》、《我的生活》、《我的老师》等。本文选自于她的自传《我的生活》中的第四章，由庄绎传翻译。[1] 本文带有一定的文学色彩，注意翻译时的用词。

The most important day I remember in all my life is the one on which my teacher, Anne Mansfield Sullivan, came to me.

在我的记忆里，安妮·曼斯菲尔德·沙利文老师来的那一天，是我一生中最重要的日子。

> **注意** 定语从句句首翻译，调整全句语序；中文善于用人作为主语，而英文善于用物作为主语，在写作的时候要注意使用这个方法。

I am filled with wonder when I consider the immeasurable contrast

---

[1] 庄绎传（1933年7月—），男，汉族，山东济南人，中共党员，教授。毕业于北京外国语学院英语系（1954年本科毕业，1957年研究生毕业）。现任北京外国语大学高级翻译学院教授、中国翻译工作者协会理事、文学艺术翻译委员会委员、《中国翻译》编委。长期从事翻译实践和教学工作，曾参加毛泽东、周恩来、刘少奇著作英译本的翻译和修订工作以及国内重要文件的英译工作，并在国内外参加联合国文件的汉译及审定工作。曾在英国、美国、法国、澳大利亚等地工作或从事学术研究。著有《汉英翻译五百例》、《英汉翻译教程》、节译After Babel（《通天塔——文学翻译理论研究》），合译The Woman in White（《白衣女人》），East Lynne（《东林怨》），Gone with the Wind（《飘》）。汉译David Copperfield（《大卫·科波菲尔》）。于1992年享受政府特殊津贴。

between the two lives which it connects.

从这一天开始，我的生活和以前迥然不同，一想到这一点，我就感到非常兴奋。

> **注意** I am filled with wonder是评论，所以放在句末翻译；when引起的句子是事实，所以放在前面翻译；定语从句可以考虑意译。

It was the third of March, 1887, three months before I was seven years old.

这个重要的日子是1887年3月3日，我差三个月不满七周岁。

> **注意** it在这里指代"这个重要的日子"，代词指明要点；后面before的译法很巧妙，不要翻译为"在……之前"。

On the afternoon of that eventful day, I stood on the porch, dumb, expectant.

在那个重要的下午，我一声不响，怀着期待的心情站在门廊里。

> **注意** 本句中两个形容词dumb和expectant，可以处理为两个形容词短语，先说主语，再说辅助语。

I guessed vaguely from my mother's signs and from the hurrying to and fro in the house that something unusual was about to happen, so I went to the door and waited on the steps.

母亲给我打着手势，人们在屋里匆匆地走来走去，我模模糊糊地预感到一件不寻常的事就要发生了，于是我就走到门口，站在台阶上等着。

> **注意** 这句话的重点是前后句的顺序，什么先发生，什么后发生，需要认真体会；from后面的短语是原因，I guessed是结果，因果关系很明确，所以翻译时要注意顺序。

The afternoon sun penetrated the mass of honeysuckle that covered the porch, and fell on my upturned face.

午后的阳光透过门廊上覆盖着的厚厚的一层忍冬，照在我微微仰着的脸上。

> **注意** 定语从句较短前置译法；honeysuckle是"忍冬"，就是"金银花"。

My fingers lingered almost unconsciously on the familiar leaves and blossoms which had just come forth to greet the sweet southern spring.

我几乎是无意识地用手抚摸着我所熟悉的叶片和花朵，这新长的叶片和刚开的花朵在南方迎来了芬芳的春天。

> **注意** finger是"手指"，但是翻译为"手"，指代整体；定语从句多于8个单词采用后置译法，且需翻译关系词"which"；定语southern翻译为状语"在南方"，定语和状语互换。

I did not know what the future held of marvel or surprise for me.

但不知今后等待着我的是什么，会让我欣喜，还是惊骇。

> **注意** 过去分词held的翻译；marvel和surprise两个抽象名词变为动词。

Anger and bitterness had preyed upon me continually for weeks and a deep languor had succeeded this passionate struggle.

几个星期以来，我又气又恨，感到非常苦恼，这种感情上的激烈斗争过去之后，我感到浑身无力。

> **注意** 中文善于用人和人体器官做主语，英文用物做主语，所以and前面的翻译要用"我"做主语；passionate struggle是"事实"，后面翻译languor表示"评论"，也是一种感情，这句话的形容十分好，看出了海伦·凯勒的文学功底。

Have you ever been at sea in a dense fog, when it seemed as if a tangible white darkness shut you in, and the great ship, tense and anxious, groped her way toward the shore with plummet and sounding-line and you waited with beating heart for something to happen?

不知你是否有过这样的经历？——在海上航行遇上了大雾，周围一片白，好像着实把你关在一个黑暗的地方，大船上的人又紧张又着急，一面用铅锤探测深浅，一面向岸边慢慢驶去，你的心也怦怦直跳，生怕出事。

> **注意** 这是个长问句，一定要将前面短句或是后面短句翻译为问句，不能翻译为一个长问句，所以在前面加上"不知"两字，后面加上"这样的经历"管住全句；white和darkness两个词有矛盾，所以翻译为两个短语，很合适；the great ship要表示"船上的人"，而不是"船"；with可以表示"一边"和"一边"的行为。

I was like that ship before my education began, only I was without compass or sounding-line, and had no way of knowing how near the harbour was.

我在开始受教育之前，就像这样一条船，只是没有罗盘，没有测深绳，也无法知道离海港有多远。

> **注意** 中文善于用人做主语，所以以"我"来起句；还有near的翻译，是"远"还是"近"，相对范畴词，中文就大不就小，中文问"有多远"或是"有多近"都用"有多远"，英文则根据实际情况来用。

"Light! Give me light!" was the wordless cry of my soul, and the light of love shone on me in that very hour.

"光明！给我光明！"这就是发自我内心深处的无言的呼唤，也就在这时候，爱心的光芒照到了我的身上。

> **注意** wordless表示"无言的"；后面的时间状语提到前面翻译，体现笔译的特点；me是"我的身上"而不是"我"，需要具体化翻译。

我和文学　My Life and Literature

本文作者是巴金，原名李尧棠，现代文学家、出版家、翻译家，同时也被誉为是"五四"新文化运动以来最有影响的作家之一，是20世纪中国杰出的文学大师、中国当代文坛的巨匠。本文是1980年巴金先生访问日本时的一段演讲，选自于《巴金文集》第十卷，由Don J. Cohn翻译。本文属于典型的文学作品，用词较难。

前两天有一位日本作家问我："你怎么同时喜欢各种流派的作家和作品呢？"

Unit 1　Stories　　15

　　A few days ago, a Japanese author asked me how I was able to appreciate authors and books of so many different schools.

> 注意　"前两天"是泛指，不是确指，所以翻译为a few days；"流派"翻译为schools；核心谓语是"喜欢"，翻译为appreciate。

　　我说："我不是文学家，不属于任何派别，所以我不受限制。"
　　I replied, "I am not 'a man of letters', nor do I belong to any particular school. Thus I was not restricted in any way."

> 注意　"文学家"翻译为a man of letters，也可以是writer；"既不……也不……"翻译为not...nor...；后面"所以"这句可以单独翻译为一个句子，因为和前面没有什么逻辑关系，合在一起翻译就会显得句子过长。

　　那位朋友又问："你明明写了那么多作品，怎么说不是文学家呢？"
　　Then he asked me, "You've written many, many books. How can you say you're not a man of letters?"

> 注意　"那位朋友"和上文重复，中文善于重复或是省略，英文善于用代词，所以翻译为he；"明明"这个词是个叠状词，在英文翻译时处理为"many, many"，前后对应，而没有把"那么多"翻译为so many。

　　我说："唯其不是文学家，我就不受文学规律的限制，我也不怕别人把我赶出文学界。"

I replied, "As long as I'm not a man of letters, I'm not subject to any of the rules of literature. Nor do I have to be afraid of being thrown out of any literary circles."

> **注意** "唯其"表示"只要",翻译为as long as;"既不……也不……"翻译为not...nor...,注意后面翻译时需要引起部分倒装。

我的敌人是什么呢?我说过:"一切旧的传统观念,一切阻止社会进步和人性发展的不合理的制度,一切摧残爱的努力,它们都是我最大的敌人。"

What are my enemies? "All outmoded traditional thinking; any irrational system which obstructs social progress or human development; any force which tramples on love——all these things are my enemies."

> **注意** 引号里的句子,需要考虑定语的翻译,"旧的"没有翻译为old,而是outmoded;第二个定语考虑要用定语从句和定语相结合;最后"它们"可以翻译为all these things,作为总结。

我所有的作品都是写来控诉、揭露、攻击这些敌人的。

All my books were written with the express purpose of denouncing, exposing and striking out at these enemies of mine.

> **注意** 这句话"写来"后面是目的,译者处理为with the express purpose of,而不是用to这个简单地表示目的的词,而且the...of也是一个抽象名词的译法,较静态化;最后增mine这个单词,表示范围。

从1929年到1948年这二十年中间,我写得快,也写得多。

In the twenty years between 1929 and 1948, I wrote very quickly and wrote a great deal.

> **注意** 数字的翻译，中英文里阿拉伯数字不变，可以直译；"写得多，写得快"形成并列结构。

我觉得有一根鞭子在抽打我的心，又觉得仿佛有什么鬼魂借我的笔为自己申冤一样。

I felt as if my mind was being whipped, as if a ghost had commandeered my pen and was writing to redress the injustices it had suffered.

> **注意** 中文善于用主动，英文善于用被动，所以"一根鞭子在抽打我的心"翻译为被动语态，whip表示"用鞭子抽打"；"借"翻译为commandeer，表示"征用"；"为"应该是目的，但是翻译为并列结构and；"申冤"翻译为redress the injustice，整个句子用词较难。

我常常同主人公一起哭笑，又常常绝望地乱搔头发。

I both cried and laughed along with my principal characters, and often despondently scratched my head.

> **注意** "哭笑"形成并列结构，所以翻译为cried and laughed；"搔头发"这是中文的表达法，因为中文善于具体，但是在英文中没有"搔头发"，只有"挠头"，所以翻译为scratched my head，而且要注意增出代词my。

我说我写作如同在生活，又说作品的最高境界是写作同生活的一致，是作家同人的一致，主要的意思是不说谎。

When I say that I write like I live, and that the highest ideal a work of literature can attain is to be at one with life, and that an author should be able to identify with his readers, I basically mean that books and their authors should never tell lies.

> **注意** "我说"后面有三个并列的句型，所以用that连接；句子中代词的使用是一个亮点，I的使用十分频繁；"作家同人"这里的"人"是"读者"，不是一般意义上的"人"；最后通过说的话而得出结论——"不说谎"，但是缺少主语，不是"我"不说谎，而是books and their authors；这句话的亮点就是代词的用法。

我最近还在另一个地方说过：艺术的最高境界是无技巧。

I've also said recently on another occasion that the highest state to which art can attain is artlessness.

> **注意** "另一个地方"并不是具体的地点，而是一种场合，所以翻译为another occasion；"艺术的"三个字处理为定语从句，而不是定语，这样可以让整个句子的定语前后平衡分配。

我几十年前同一位朋友辩论时就说过："长得好看的人用不着浓妆艳抹，而我的文章就像一个丑八怪，不打扮，看起来倒还顺眼些。"

When I was arguing this point with a friend several decades ago, I said, "Physically attractive people don't need heavy make-up. Though my writing resembles an ugly monster, it actually looks a little better without any embellishment."

> **注意** "长相好看的人"不用beauty,因为这样的人实在少见,还是用physically attractive people比较合适;"浓妆艳抹"可以翻译为"浓妆"或是"艳抹";后面三个小句子的逻辑关系很重要,though可以表示微弱的转折关系,还和后面的句子形成让步关系,这个单词的用法既是转折,也是让步。

他说:"流传久远的作品是靠文学技巧流传,谁会关心百十年前的生活?"

His reply was, "Literary works have stood the test of time because of the skill with which they were written. Who today really cares about the details of what life was like a hundred years ago?"

> **注意** "他说"表示对前面话的回应,所以翻译为his reply;"流传久远的作品"偏正短语主谓译法,所以是"作品流传久远";"是靠"表示原因;后面这句和前面的句子没有逻辑上的关系,所以进行分译,不需要用and连接。

我不同意,我认为打动人心的还是作品中所反映的生活和主人公的命运。

I disagree. Readers are moved by the life reflected in a story and the fate of the chief characters.

> **注意** 前后两个句子逻辑上没有关系,所以分译,用句号连接;"我认为"和前面表示观点句子重复,可以不翻译;然而后面句子缺少真正主语,所以寻找隐藏主语,把readers作为句子的真正主语,"打动人心的"改变为宾语;这个句子重点在主语和谓语的处理上,比较难。

这仍然是在反对那些无中生有、混淆黑白的花言巧语。

This means I oppose fabrication, deception and flowery language.

注意 "无中生有"可以理解为"编造",所以是fabrication;"混淆黑白的花言巧语"可以理解为"混淆黑白和花言巧语","混淆黑白"可以理解为deception。

我最恨那些盗名欺世、欺骗读者的谎言。

What I hate most are those glory-seeking writers who deceive the public with their lies.

注意 "我最恨"翻译为What I hate most比I hate更加静态,更加符合英语的特点;"盗名欺世、欺骗读者的谎言"直接翻译为glory-seeking lies不通顺,所以翻译为glory-seeking writers,后面再跟定语从句,这样比较灵活。

Unit 2

History

England Before the Industrial Revolution
工业革命前的英国

本文作者是雅各布·布罗诺夫斯基,英国著名学者,编写的《人类的发展》是著名的电视系列片。本文选自第八章,由吴千之翻译。[1]本文是典型的非文学翻译,翻译现象体现得较为明显。

The country was a place where men worked from dawn to dark, and the labourer lived not in the sun, but in poverty and darkness.

在农村,人们从早到晚都得干活,劳动者并不是沐浴在阳光下,而是生活在贫困和黑暗之中。

注意 where引导的定语从句没有翻译为定语,而是翻译为状语,这称为定状互换的译法;from dawn to dark 表示"从早到晚";lived not in... but in...翻译为"不是沐浴在……而是生活在……",遵循了动词分配的原则。

What aids there were to lighten labour were immemorial, like the mill, which was already ancient in Chaucer's time.

---

[1] 吴千之,北京外国语大学英语学院教授,著名学者,曾在美国哈佛大学执教。

那些帮助减轻劳动的机械都不知从哪个年代起就有了，比如磨坊，在乔叟的时代就已经是古老的了。

注意 what指的是下文中mill等机械，所以代词指明要点；What aids there were to lighten labour=the aids that had been invented to lighten labaour是主语；后面定语从句后置，虽然少于8个单词，但是是用来修饰单一成分的，放在前面翻译，句子就不通顺了。

The Industrial Revolution began with such machines; the millwrights were the engineers of the coming age.

而产业革命就是从这些机械开始的。修造磨坊的匠人就是开创新时代的工程师。

注意 英文中的分号可以相当于中文的句号；engineer可以认为是抽象名词，所以在翻译时增动词"开创"。

James Brindley of Staffordshire started his self-made career in 1733 by working at mill wheels, at the age of seventeen, having been born poor in a village.

斯塔福郡的詹姆斯·布林德雷，出生于一个贫苦的农村家庭；1733年，他十七岁，就着手改良磨坊的车轮，从而开始了他那自我奋斗的生涯。

注意 这句话的特点是从句翻译时的顺序，这是高级笔译所涉及的内容，中文按照时间先后的顺序进行表达，而英文则是根据句子所要强调的顺序进行安排句序，重要的是主句，次要的则是从句或是分词等。

Unit 2　History

Brindley's improvements were practical to sharpen and step up the performance of the water wheel as a machine.

布林德雷所做出的改良是很实际的：改善并加强水车的机械功能。

注意 improvements可以理解为抽象名词，所以增词；performance可以和后面的as a machine同时理解为机械功能，这里特别要注意performance表示"功能"，而不是"表演"，背单词的时候要注意一个单词的所有用法，而不仅仅是核心含义。

It was the first multi-purpose machine for the new industries.

这是为新工业提供的第一部多功能机器。

注意 it在这里指代上文中的water wheel，所以翻译为"这"，而不是"它"，当然也可以翻译为"水车"；machine在冠词之后，介词之前，可以理解为抽象名词，所以增词"提供"。

Brindley worked, for example, to improve the grinding of flints, which were used in the rising pottery industry.

例如，布林德雷努力改进燧石的碾磨过程，燧石是新兴的陶瓷工业有用的材料。

注意 插入语表示观点时需要提到句首翻译；grinding是典型的抽象名词，有动词词根时，翻译为动词"研磨"；后面还可以增词"过程"，这是一个范畴词；后面的非限定性定语从句需要翻译关系词，而且翻译非限定性定语从句时一定要用后置译法。

Yet there was a bigger movement in the air by 1750.

而到了1750年，一场更大的运动已经在酝酿之中。

> **注意** yet表示微弱的转折，所以翻译为"而"；后面的in the air 表示"酝酿当中"，不是表示"在空气当中"。

Water had become the engineers' element, and men like Brindley were possessed by it.

水成了工程师们大显身手的对象，像布林德雷这样的人对它都着了迷。

> **注意** the engineers' element相当于the right thing for engineers；possessed相当于strongly influenced；men like Brindley翻译为"像布林德雷这样的人"，英文先总后分，中文先分后总。

Water was gushing and fanning out all over the countryside. It was not simply a source of power, it was a new wave of movement.

水在农村到处涌流漫溢，它不仅是一种能源，而且带来了一场新的运动。

> **注意** 前后两句关系紧密，而且是短句，可以考虑用合并译法；后一句中的it可以翻译为代词，因为在前面已经提到过"水"；后两句中间没有连词，实际上在语法上有些问题，但是句子包括一正一反两个短句时，是可以不用连词的；simply表示only"仅仅，只是"的意思。

James Brindley was a pioneer in the art of building canals or, as it was then called, 'navigation'.

Unit 2　History　25

詹姆斯·布林德雷是开凿运河的先驱者，当时人们把开凿运河叫做"navigation"。

> **注意** art是一个抽象名词，抽象名词有很多种翻译方法，在这里可以不翻译；it was called翻译为"人们叫做"；后面navigation是中间语言，可以不翻译，这是唯一一种不翻译的情况，中间语言指的是其他语种，或是用于解释前面语言的单词。

Brindley had begun on his own account, out of interest, to survey the waterways that he travelled as he went about his engineering projects for mills and mines.

布林德雷在为他的磨坊和矿井建筑工程到处奔走的时候，出于自愿和兴趣，对沿途经过的河道进行了勘察。

> **注意** 先翻译主语，然后翻译as后面的句子；on one's own account表示"出于自愿"；out of interest表示"出于兴趣"；最后一个定语从句可以前置译法。

The Duke of Bridgewater then got him to build a canal to carry coal from the Duke's pits at Worsley to the rising town of Manchester…

于是布里奇瓦特公爵就让他开一条运河，以便把煤从公爵在乌斯利拥有的矿井运往新兴城市曼彻斯特……

> **注意** then时间状语放在句首翻译；get sb. to do sth.表示"让某人做某事"；pits表示"矿井"；rising town表示"新兴城市"。

Brindley went on to connect Manchester with Liverpool in an even bolder manner, and in all laid out almost four hundred miles of canals in a network all over England.

布林德雷还更加大胆地用运河把曼彻斯特同利物浦联结起来，修凿了总长度为四百英里的遍布全英国的运河网。

> **注意** 先说主语，再说状语，最后说最主要的内容；这里增了一个对象词——"用运河"，这是上下文的增词；laid out表示"修凿"；canals in a network表示"运河网"。

Two things are outstanding in the creation of the English system of canals, and they characterize all the Industrial Revolution.

有两点在修建英国运河网的过程中非常突出，而这两点也正是整个产业革命的特点。

> **注意** creation是典型的抽象名词，翻译为动词；后面的characterize在中文里没有对应词，所以应该意译，或者是翻译为其他词性；the Industrial Revolution翻译为"产业革命"。

One is that the men who made the revolution were practical men.

首先，发动这场革命的都是些实干家。

> **注意** one不要翻译为"一个"，而是"首先"和"其次"；the men were…men有同指现象，所以只翻译一次；后面的定语从句采取前置译法；practical men翻译为"实干家"。

Like Brindley, they often had little education, and in fact school education as it then was could only dull an inventive mind.

同布林德雷一样，他们一般都没有受过什么教育，事实上，当时那种学校教育也只能窒息人的创造性。

> **注意** as it then was相当于as it was at that time,是一个定语从句,修饰前面的school education;dull这个单词本来是形容词,在这里作为动词,表示"make...dull";inventive mind注意有词性转换,inventive变成了名词"创造性"。

The grammar schools legally could only teach the classical subjects for which they had been founded.

按规定,文法学校只能讲授古典学科,这些学校的办学宗旨本来就是如此。

> **注意** legally属于较长形容词或是副词,可以提到句首,翻译为小句子;后面定语从句的翻译要注意前置还是后置,原本句子很短应该前置,但是代词较多,为了让它更加明确,所以放在后面,they指的是这些学校,而which指的是前面那些课程。

The universities also (there were only two, at Oxford and Cambridge) took little interest in modern or scientific studies; and they were closed to those who did not conform to the Church of England.

大学(当时只有两所,一所在牛津,一所在剑桥)对现代的或科学的学科也不怎么感兴趣,这两所大学还把不信奉英国国教的人关在门外。

> **注意** 前面的标点符号仍然保留;代词they需要指明要点;后面的定语从句少于8个单词,所以前置;those who不翻译为"那些人",就是"……的人"即可;the Church of England表示"英国国教"。

The other outstanding feature is that the new inventions were for everyday use.

第二个突出的特点是：新发明都是为日常生活服务的。

> **注意** 这里的The other是和前面文章的one相对应的，所以翻译为"第二个"；everyday和every day是有区别的，前者表示"日常的"，后者表示"每天"。

The canals were arteries of communication: They were not made to carry pleasure boats, but barges.

运河是交通的动脉，开凿运河不是为了通行游艇，而是为了通行驳船。

> **注意** they是指代什么，原本指代句中的"运河"，但是如果翻译为"运河"，后面的被动语态就不好翻译了，所以将这个单词具体化，翻译为"开凿运河"；pleasure boats表示"游艇"；后面的"驳船"前面需要增一个动词"通行"，这是翻译中动词分配的原则。

And the barges were not made to carry luxuries, but pots and pans and bales of cloth, boxes of ribbon, and all the common things that people buy by the pennyworth.

而驳船也不是为了运送奢侈品，而是为了运送瓦罐铁锅、成包的棉布、成箱的缎带，以及那些只花个把便士就能买到的各式日用品。

> **注意** 前面的被动语态和上句的处理方式一样；but后面的名词前增动词，遵守动词的分配原则；最后一个定语从句少于8个单词，所以可以前置翻译。

These things had been manufactured in villages which were growing into towns now, away from London; it was a country-wide trade.

这些物品都是在远离伦敦渐渐发展成为城镇的农村制造的。这是一场全国范围的贸易。

注意 前面被动语态的译法，可以用"是……的"结构翻译；而且中间的定语从句少于8个单词，所以可以采用前置译法；进行时态可以翻译为"渐渐"，表示近期一直在发生的动作；最后的分号相当于句号。

Opportunities Open in the West　西部地区的开发机会

本文选自于An Outline of American History，是美国国务院国际信息局出版物，由美国多所大学教授共同编写，对于普及美国历史知识很有帮助，在美国大使馆网站上有完整版。本文选自于其中的第二章，属于典型的非文学翻译，翻译现象较多。

The first great rush of population to the far west was drawn to the mountainous regions, where gold was found in California in 1848, in Colorado and Nevada ten years later, in Montana and Wyoming in the 1860s, and in the Black Hills of the Dakota country in the 1870s.

最初大规模迁往极西地带的移民，大多集中在山区。在那里，加州于1848年发现了金矿，十年后在科罗拉多和内华达州，十九世纪六十年代在蒙大拿和怀俄明州，十九世纪七十年代在达科他的黑山地区都先后发现了金矿。

> **注意** 本句地点比较多，要注意美国地点的翻译；第一个被动语态使用了"有被不用被"的译法；后面的被动语态同样用此方法；中文先说次要内容"……（地点）"，将重要内容"发现金矿"放在最后说。

Miners opened up the country, established communities and laid the foundations for more permanent settlements.

采矿者开发了这些地区，建立了村镇，打下了永久定居的基础。

> **注意** 这个句子没有难点，但是permanent settlements的翻译，应该翻译为"永久定居"才更加合适。

Yet even while digging in the hills, some settlers perceived the region's farming and stock-raising possibilities.

不过，在山区采矿的同时，有些移民已看到这些地区有从事农业和畜牧业的可能。

> **注意** yet表示微弱的转折，所以翻译为"不过"；perceived表示"观察"，可以翻译为"看到"；possibilities为典型的抽象名词，所以可以增词"从事"。

Eventually, though a few communities continued to be devoted almost exclusively to mining, the real wealth of Montana, Colorado, Wyoming, Idaho, and California proved to be in the grass and soil.

后来，少数城镇虽然专门从事采矿业，但蒙大拿、科罗拉多、怀俄明、爱达荷等州的真正财富，也和加州一样，还是在草原和沃

Unit 2　History

土中。

> **注意** continued to be devoted这个可以理解为"动词的过渡"，前面是弱势动词，所以不翻译；中文关联词双双出现，后面增上"但是"；proved to be翻译为"是"，为系表结构。

Cattle-raising, long an important industry in Texas, became even more flourishing after the war, when enterprising men began to drive their Texas longhorns north across the open public domain.

在德克萨斯州，养牛早就是重要事业，战后尤见繁荣。大胆的赶牛人赶着德州的长角牛，穿过开放的公共地带，向北走去。

> **注意** 先说主语，再说次要内容；前面同位语可以翻译为主谓结构；后面句子中的north提出来最后翻译，译为"向北走去"。

Feeding as they went, the cattle arrived at railway shipping points in Kansas, larger and fatter than when they started.

牛群边走边吃，到堪萨斯州的铁路运输站时，已长得比出发时更大更肥壮了。

> **注意** 分词位于句首，先找主语，翻译主语；railway shipping points表示"铁路运输站"，而不是"铁路船运站"；后面they可以省略不翻译，中文善于用名词或是省略，英文善于用代词。

Soon this "long drive" became a regular event, and, or hundreds of kilometers, trails were dotted with herds of cattle moving northward.

不久，这样的"长征"就成为常事了。向北移动的牛群，在几百公里的征途上，留下了无数的足迹。

> **注意** long drive翻译为"长征";后面的被动语态翻译成为主动形式;moving northward是定语,用来修饰cattle;注意,"and,"这个形式很有意思,可以想想和",and"这个结构有什么区别,",and"的翻译也是一个很有意思的话题。

Cattle-raising spread into the trans-Missouri region, and immense ranches appeared in Colorado, Wyoming, Kansas, Nebraska, and the Dakota territory.

养牛业迅速超出了密苏里地区,在科罗拉多、怀俄明、堪萨斯、内布拉斯加和达科他等地区,都出现了巨大的牧场。

> **注意** trans-前缀的意思是"转换",在这里处理为动词"超越";后面的地点状语需要提到句首翻译;ranches表示"农场"。

Western cities flourished as centers for the slaughter and dressing of meat.

西部城市因成为屠宰业和调制肉类的中心而繁荣起来。

> **注意** as在这里表示原因;先说主语再说次要内容;center可以理解为抽象名词,所以可以在翻译的时候增动词;dressing of meat表示"调制肉类"。

Altogether, between 1866 and 1888, some six million head of cattle were driven up from Texas to winters on the high plains of Colorado, Wyoming, and Montana.

在1866年至1888年间,大约有六百万头牛从德州放牧到科罗拉

Unit 2 History 33

多、怀俄明、蒙大拿等地的高原上过冬。

注意 some可以表示"大约";winter可以转化词性为动词,表示"过冬";to是介词,后面跟的是名词;to winter在翻译时要放在最后;被动语态用"有被不用被"的译法。

The cattle boom reached its height by 1885, then the range became too heavily pastured to support the long drive, and was beginning to be criss-crossed by railroads.

养牛业的兴旺发达,到1885年已达到最高峰,当时的高原,已经不足以供这么多长征牛群吃草的需要了,而且这些草原也开始为纵横交错的铁路线所割裂。

注意 首先主谓结构的偏正译法;then在这里表示at that time;and后面缺主语,所以需要增主语;最后的被动语态用"为……所"结构翻译。

Not far behind the rancher creaked the prairie schooners of the farmers bringing their families, their draft horses, cows, and pigs.

在牧牛人身后不远之外,有许多草原篷车在吱吱作响,农民把他们的妻儿,还有拉车的马、奶牛和猪群也带了来。

注意 这句话的断句很重要,因为再短的句子也需要有逗号;在of处断句是很好的选择;后面的句子直接处理为主谓结构;their物主代词出现第二次时不用翻译。

Under the Homestead Act they staked their claims and fenced them with barbed wire.

根据《宅地法》，他们圈定了所得的土地，并用铁蒺藜围起来。

> **注意** the Homestead Act表示"宅地法"；claims表示"所得的土地"，reclaim表示"开垦土地"；barbed wire表示"铁蒺藜"；介词with翻译为动词。

Ranchmen were ousted from lands they had roamed without legal title. Soon the romantic "wild west" had ceased to be.

原来未经合法手续取得土地的牧牛人都被赶了出去。不久，这片具有浪漫气氛的"西部荒原"，便不复存在了。

> **注意** 前面句子的顺序，定语从句的句首译法，所以要调整全句语序；romantic可以理解为抽象形容词，所以增词，既增动词，又增范畴词，让句子更加通顺。

新民主主义论　On New Democracy

本文选自于《毛泽东选集》第二卷，由钱钟书主持翻译，[1]属于典型的非文学作品，其中句型结构和用词都十分讲究。

五四运动是反帝国主义的运动，又是反封建的运动。

---

[1] 钱钟书，原名仰先，字哲良，中国现代著名作家、文学研究家。曾为《毛泽东选集》英文版翻译小组成员。晚年就职于中国社会科学院，任副院长。书评家夏志清先生认为小说《围城》是"中国近代文学中最有趣、最用心经营的小说，可能是最伟大的一部"。钱钟书在文学、国学、比较文学和文化批评等领域的成就卓著，推崇者甚至冠以"钱学"。

Unit 2　History

The May 4th Movement was an anti-imperialist as well as an anti-feudal movement.

> **注意**　"五四运动"翻译为The May 4th Movement；中文里两次出现"是"这个动词，英文善于用省略，所以动词只翻译一次；"又"可以用连接词as well as，相当于and；"反帝国主义"是"反对帝国主义者"；两次出现的"运动"只翻译一次，遵守定语的分配原则。

五四运动的杰出的历史意义，在于它带着为辛亥革命还不曾有的姿态，这就是彻底地不妥协地反帝国主义和彻底地不妥协地反封建主义。

Its outstanding historical significance is to be seen in a feature which was absent from the Revolution of 1911, namely, its thorough and uncompromising opposition to imperialism as well as to feudalism.

> **注意**　第一个名词在上文中提到，所以翻译为代词，英文善于用代词；"这就是"翻译为namely；"彻底地不妥协地"出现两次，只需要翻译一次，英文不需要重复；"反"本身为动词，翻译为名词，英文是静态性语言。

五四运动所以具有这种性质，是在当时中国的资本主义经济已有进一步的发展，当时中国的革命知识分子眼见得俄、德、奥三大帝国主义国家已经瓦解，英、法两大帝国主义国家已经受伤，而俄国无产阶级已经建立了社会主义国家，德、奥（匈牙利）、意三国无产阶级在革命中，因而发生了中国民族解放的新希望。

The May 4th Movement possessed this quality because capitalism had developed a step further in China and because new hopes had arisen for the liberation of the Chinese nation as China's revolutionary intellectuals saw the collapse of three great imperialist powers, Russia, Germany and Austria-Hungary, and the weakening of two others, Britain and France, while the Russian proletariat had established a socialist state and the German, Hungarian and Italian proletariat had risen in revolution.

> **注意** 这句话可以说是本书最难的句子，首先"是在当时中国的资本主义经济已有进一步的发展"和"因而发生了中国民族解放的新希望"是第一句子的原因，所以把最后一句放在了第三句来翻译；as表示"当时中国……"的所有内容，表示"因而"的原因；"已经瓦解"、"受伤"用的是抽象名词翻译；"而"表示承接对照关系，所以翻译为while；"已经建立"可以翻译为过去完成时，表示在这些所有动作之前发生；特别要注意每个分句之间的关系，用连词连接，中文是意合语言，英文是形合语言。

五四运动是在当时世界革命号召之下，是在俄国革命号召之下，是在列宁号召之下发生的。

The May 4th Movement came into being at the call of the world revolution, of the Russian Revolution and of Lenin.

> **注意** 这个句子只有一个难点，"在……号召之下"出现三次，中文善于重复，而英文善于省略，所以这个短语只需要出现一次；核心动词"是"，可以翻译为came into being。

五四运动是当时无产阶级世界革命的一部分。

It was part of the world proletarian revolution of the time.

Unit 2　History

> **注意**　"五四运动"已经在前面出现过，所以在这里用代词，英文善于用代词；part of这个短语前面不用冠词；"当时"翻译为the time。

五四运动时期虽然还没有中国共产党，但是已经有了大批的赞成俄国革命的具有初步共产主义思想的知识分子。

Although the Communist Party of China had not yet come into existence, there were already large numbers of intellectuals who approved of the Russian Revolution and had the rudiments of communist ideology.

> **注意**　第一个分句的主语是什么；句子中用"但是"，其在翻译时在句首用了although；后面的分句中有三个定语，不能全部处理为前置定语，而是要有前有后，形成前后平衡的状态；"赞成俄国革命的具有初步共产主义思想的"实际上是两个并列结构。

五四运动，在其开始，是共产主义的知识分子、革命的小资产阶级知识分子和资产阶级知识分子（他们是当时运动中的右翼）三部分人的统一战线的革命运动。

In the beginning the May 4th Movement was the revolutionary movement of a united front of three sections of people——communist intellectuals, revolutionary petty-bourgeois intellectuals and bourgeois intellectuals (the last forming the right wing of the movement).

> **注意**　时间状语需要放在句首翻译；中文先分后总，英文先总后分，所以翻译时先说"三部分"，再翻译是哪三部分；这句话中有很多专有名词，记住这些词的表达方法。

它的弱点，就在只限于知识分子，没有工人农民参加。

Its shortcoming was that it was confined to the intellectuals and that the workers and peasants did not join in.

> **注意** "只限于"翻译为被动语态；后面两个句子之间可以认为是并列关系，所以用and连接。

但发展到六三运动时，就不但是知识分子，而且有广大的无产阶级、小资产阶级和资产阶级参加，成了全国范围的革命运动了。

But as soon as it developed into the June 3rd Movement, not only the intellectuals but the mass of the proletariat, the petty bourgeoisie and the bourgeoisies joined in, and it became a nation-wide revolutionary movement.

> **注意** 这些分句之间的关系，需要在第一个句子前面加上as soon as表示时间关系；最后一个分句和前面这些句子之间是并列关系，所以用and进行连接；特别要注意句中"无产阶级"、"小资产阶级"和"资产阶级"的翻译。

五四运动所进行的文化革命则是彻底地反对封建文化的运动，自有中国历史以来，还没有过这样伟大而彻底的文化革命。

The cultural revolution ushered in by the May 4th Movement was uncompromising in its opposition to feudal culture; there had never been such a great and thoroughgoing cultural revolution since the dawn of Chinese history.

> **注意** "所进行的"用ushered in这个过去分词来进行表达；"反对"用静态的名词来翻译；两个句子之间要有连接，没有连接用

Unit 2 History 39

分号;"自有中国历史以来"用静态的名词结构来进行翻译,处理为the dawn of Chinese history。

当时以反对旧道德提倡新道德,反对旧文学提倡新文学,为文化革命的两大旗帜,立下了伟大的功劳。

Raising aloft the two great banners of the day, "Down with the old ethics and up with the new!" and "Down with the old literature and up with the new!", the cultural revolution had great achievements to its credit.

注意 前面两小句的"反对"和"提倡"处理为介词,而不是动词;原句无主语,"文化革命"成为主语,偏正短语取偏做主语,前半句用一个现在分词,说明它具体的事情,后半句说明其意义;中文先分后总,英文先总后分。

这个文化运动,当时还没有可能普及到工农群众中去。

At that time it was not yet possible for this cultural movement to become widely diffused among the workers and peasants.

注意 中文先说主语,英文先翻译状语;这句话口译和笔译有很大区别,笔译在于重点强调"没有可能",所以用it was not yet possible的结构;"普及"翻译为become widely diffused。

它提出了"平民文学"口号,但是当时的所谓"平民",实际上还只能限于城市小资产阶级和资产阶级的知识分子,即所谓市民阶级的知识分子。

The slogan of "Literature for the Common People" was advanced, but in fact the "common people" then could only refer to the petty-bourgeois and bourgeois intellectuals in the cities, that is, the urban intelligentsia.

> **注意** 第一个分句使用了被动语态，英文善于使用被动语态；"仅限于"可以翻译为only refer to；两个分句之间需要连接，中文可以用逗号隔开，但是英文需要连接，"即"翻译为that is。

五四运动是在思想上和干部上准备了一九二一年中国共产党的成立，又准备了五卅运动和北伐战争。

Both in ideology and in the matter of cadres, the May 4th Movement paved the way for the founding of the Chinese Communist Party in 1921 and for the May 30th Movement in 1925 and the Northern Expedition.

> **注意** 英文先翻译状语，再翻译主语；"为……做准备"翻译为paved the way for；"五卅运动"和"北伐战争"属于专有名词翻译。

当时的资产阶级知识分子，是五四运动的右翼，到了第二个时期，他们中间的大部分就和敌人妥协，站在反动方面了。

The bourgeois intellectuals, who constituted the right wing of the May 4th Movement, mostly compromised with the enemy in the second period and went over to the side of reaction.

> **注意** 这句话的难点在于确定主要谓语是什么；把"资产阶级知识分子"和后面的"他们"只翻译一次，这个处理得很妥当，而且只有一个主语；把"是"这个谓语翻译为非限定性定语从句；最后一个逗号之间翻译为and。

Geography

Unit 3

Journey Up the Nile 沿尼罗河而上

本文作者罗伯特·卡普托，美国《国家地理》杂志的摄影记者。本文选自美国《国家地理》杂志，由庄绎传翻译。本文属于写实的写作手法，既有文学的对话和描写，也有非文学的阐述，所以翻译时需要注意句子的结构和用词的方法。

Egypt, wrote the Greek historian Hecataeus, is the gift of the Nile.
希腊历史学家赫卡泰奥斯写道：埃及是尼罗河送来的礼物。

> 注意 插入语表示观点，需要提到句首翻译；Hecataeus是希腊著名的历史学家；the gift of是典型的抽象名词，所以增动词进行翻译。

No other country is so dependent on a single lifeline.
任何别的国家都没有这样依赖着唯一的一条生命线。

> 注意 这个句子的主语no other表示否定，而且要注意否定是完全否定还是部分否定。

Egypt's very soil was born in the Nile's annual flood with the flood came the life-giving mud that made Egypt the granary of the ancient world.

就连埃及的土地也是尼罗河每年泛滥而带来的。河水泛滥带来了泥沙，万物得以生长，埃及就这样成了古代世界的粮仓。

> **注意** very在这里成为形容词，加强语气；was born是象征性说法，翻译为"带来"；with引导的是倒装句，就是因为后面有个定语从句才倒装的；the life-giving mud相当于 mud that gives life。

And as rain fell in the Ethiopian highlands and the snows melted in the Mountains of the Moon, the river was everlastingly renewed.

埃塞俄比亚高原上的雨水，和月亮山上融化的积雪，为尼罗河提供了无穷无尽的水源。

> **注意** 为了让前面两句通顺，此处用了主谓结构的偏正译法；后面句子的被动语态翻译得很巧妙，和前面句子连接得很通顺。

"This is the best place on earth," said Ahmed, an Egyptian fellah, or farmer, I encountered in the Nile Delta, that incredibly fertile 8,500-square-mile triangle between Cairo and the Mediterranean coast.

"这是世界上最好的地方。"阿赫迈德对我说。他是我在尼罗河三角洲遇见的一位农民（当地人管农民叫"夫埃拉"）。从开罗到地中海之间这块8 500平方英里的三角地带，土地异常肥沃。

> **注意** said是及物动词，所以增对象词；同位语处理为主谓译法；定语从句较短，翻译时用前置译法；that引导的是同位语从句，和the Nile Delta形成同位语，因为和前句没有什么关系，所以翻译为另一个句子；incredibly fertile可以翻译成短句。

The delta and the narrow Nile Valley to the south make up only three percent of Egypt's land but are home to ninety-six percent of her population.

三角洲和南边狭窄的尼罗河河谷只占埃及土地的百分之三，却有百分之九十六的人口住在这里。

> 注意 be home to...为重要词组，所以翻译为"……住在这里"；make up为重要词组，翻译为"占"，这是重要的口译词汇。

Here nearly 48 million people live in an area only slightly larger than Maryland.

将近4800万人生活的这块地方只比美国马里兰州略大一点。

> 注意 这句话的难点在于要增词，Maryland对于读者来说并不知道是什么地方，所以要增范围词，增"美国"这两个字。

The rest of Egypt is desert.

埃及其余的地方全是沙漠。

> 注意 本句无难点，直接翻译。

"Truly Allah has blessed us," Ahmed exclaimed piously. "Soil, water, sun——we can grow anything!"

"真主可真是保佑我们哪，"阿赫迈德虔诚地说道，"我们有土地，有水，有阳光——种什么都行啊！"

> 注意 Truly Allah翻译为"真主安拉"；后面这句是农民的语言，所以可以比较口语化；而且在这里有几个名词，需要根据自然增词法，增"有"。

In the gathering dusk Ahmed and his five companions had invited me to join them.

天色渐渐暗了下来，阿赫迈德和五个一起干活的人早就约我去和他们玩儿。

> **注意** gathering dusk，为了让句子更加通顺，可以用偏正结构的主谓译法，所以翻译为"天色渐渐暗了下来"；had invited翻译为"早就约我"，这里的时态翻译很巧妙；join them根据后面句子的意思，翻译为"玩"。

Their galabias and turbans stained by the sweat and dirt of a long day's work, they sat in front of a wayside shop, enjoying three of the best things in life along the Nile——tea, conversation, and the water pipe.

他们干了一天活儿，袍子和头巾上又是汗，又是土。这时候，他们坐在路旁一家商店门口，享受尼罗河沿岸人们生活里的三件最大的乐事——喝茶、聊天、抽水烟。

> **注意** 第一个分句的处理方式类似于文学翻译，独立主格结构按照主谓结构翻译；最后破折号后的三个名词需要增词，属于自然增词法的一种。

At the edge of a nearby canal, donkeys laden with freshly harvested alfalfa waited for their masters to lead them home, braying a fretful counterpoint to the steady thud of an irrigation pump.

在附近的一条水渠旁，驴子背上驮着刚割的苜蓿，等着主人牵它们回家去，一面发出一阵阵急促的叫声，和浇地的水泵不断发出的突突声交织在一起。

> **注意** canal在这里表示"水渠";laden with freshly harvested属于分词结构,可以当做非限定性定语从句翻译;counterpoint是个需要认真理解的词汇,表示前后两者的对照,而且是同等地位,因为没有中文对应单词,所以需要意译;thud表示"浇地时发出的突突的声音";后面这句翻译是本句的经典。

All this suggested ancient harmonies.

这一切让人感到古代的和谐气氛。

> **注意** suggested表示"感到",不是"建议";harmonies表示"和谐",再增范畴词"气氛",这个增词很有特点。

Yet the Nile has been changed by modern man in ways not yet fully understood.

而现代的人却让尼罗河发生了变化,不过就连他们自己也不完全了解尼罗河改变的方式。

> **注意** 本句中的两个被动语态的处理是亮点,两个都用了变被动为主动的方法,而且要注意ways的理解。

In 1971 engineers and workers completed the Aswan High Dam, nearly 600 miles upriver from Cairo toward the Sudanese frontier.

1971年,技术人员和工人建成了阿斯旺高坝,这座水坝在从开罗沿尼罗河向苏丹边境走去将近六百英里远的地方。

> **注意** engineer不仅表示"工程师",也可以表示"技术人员";后面的同位语用的是主谓结构翻译。

It is the greatest public work to be undertaken in Egypt since the Pyramids.

这是埃及自从修建金字塔以来进行的一项最大的公共工程。

 这是一个强调句型，要注意后面不定式做的定语。

The devastating floods and droughts that imposed a recurrent tax of suffering on the fellahin no longer occur.

过去给农民带来灾难的水旱灾害，现在不再发生了。

 这句话很具有抽象含义，特别是tax这个单词，不是"税"；recurrent翻译为"一再发生的"；定语从句较长，原本应该采用后置译法，但是这个句子考虑到谓语的情况，所以将定语前置。

Egyptian agriculture has been transformed, and industry is benefiting from power generated by the dam.

埃及的农业得到了改造，工业也用上了水坝发出的电力。

 第一个被动语态翻译为"得到了"；benefiting from翻译为"用上了"；最后一个分词做定语，可以用前置译法。

But there have been negative effects also.

但是也有不良的后果。

 这句话中的also用法，一般来说，这个单词用在句中，但是在这里用于句末，表示"也"的意思。

Unit 3　Geography　　47

　　Standing on a sandy beach at the mouth of the Rosetta branch of the Nile, I was puzzled by what seemed a ghost town——a sad vista of crumbling buildings, smashed windows, and broken wires dangling from utility poles.

　　洛塞塔河是尼罗河入海处的一个支流，我站在河口的沙滩上看到一个小镇，感到迷惑不解。这仿佛是一个被人遗弃了的小镇，一片萧索景象，房子濒于倒塌，窗户破碎，断了的电线挂在电线杆子上。

> **注意** 分词位于句首找主语；分词中定语较多，所以先翻译，可以用偏正短语的主谓译法；主句中先陈述事实by what seemed a ghost town，后评论was puzzled；为了使后面几个短语通顺，同时使用了偏正短语的主谓译法。

　　One house teetered drunkenly, half in, half out of the sea.

　　有一所房子好像喝醉了的人一样摇摇晃晃，一半泡在海里，一半在陆地上。

> **注意** 这句话的谓语teeter表示摇摇晃晃；drunkenly是暗喻，英文是暗喻，中文无论如何都要翻译为明喻。

　　"Last summer, people stayed in those rooms——this was a summer resort," said a voice behind me.

　　"去年夏天，那所房子还有人住过——这是一个避暑胜地。"在我身后有人这样说道。

> **注意** people stayed in those rooms为了强调宾语，所以翻译时前后倒置；引号后面的主谓倒置，翻译时要用正常语序。

The speaker was a young Egyptian named Muhammad, member of a team from Alexandria that had come to this abandoned village to study coastal erosion.

说话的是一位名叫穆罕默德的埃及青年，他是一个考察队的队员，专门从亚历山大港到这个荒芜的村庄来考察沿海地区水土流失的情况。

> **注意** 第一个分句中的后置定语，可以表示定语从句，采用前置译法；后面的同位语从句，用主谓译法；最后一个定语从句较长，使用后置译法；coastal erosion表示"水土流失"，后面可以增范畴词"情况"。

"Now the sea is moving in," said Muhammad.

"海水越来越往里边来。"穆罕默德说道。

> **注意** sea表示"海水"，中文较具体，英文较抽象；后面的主谓倒置，翻译时要用正常语序。

He pointed to a lighthouse perched on a tiny island a couple of miles offshore: "That lighthouse used to be on land.

他指着坐落在离海岸二三英里的小岛上的一座灯塔说："那座灯塔本来是在陆地上的。

> **注意** 分词位于名词之后相当于定语从句，所以采用前置译法；used to be表示"过去常常是"，在这里处理为"本来"。

About six years ago it became an island.

大约六年前，那地方变成了一个小岛。

> **注意** 再短的句子也要有逗号；代词 it 翻译为具体事物，翻译为"那地方"。

Day by day the sea is eating the land——the dam has stopped the sediment of the Nile from replenishing the shoreline.

海水一天天冲刷陆地——水坝已经让尼罗河的泥沙无法沉积下来加固海岸了。

> **注意** stopped 在这里相当于 prevented；the sediment of 属于典型的抽象名词结构，中间的抽象名词翻译为动词"沉淀"。

As we chatted, a brightly painted sardine boat dropped anchor.

我们正在聊着，只见一条颜色鲜艳的捕捞沙丁鱼的船抛了锚。

> **注意** as 不要翻译为生硬的时间连接词，中文不善于用连词，属于意合语言；后面主语多个形容词修饰名词时排序的情况亦需要注意，这属于语法问题。

The captain came ashore and joined our conversation.

船长上了岸，凑过来和我们说话。

> **注意** 再短的句子也要有逗号；后面一个句子翻译得更有口语化的特点。

"Before they started the High Dam 25 years ago," he said, "the Nile mud had a lot of food in it, and so the sardines gathered near the mouth of the river to feed."

他说:"二十五年前,在修建高坝之前,尼罗河的泥沙里面有很多可吃的东西,所以沙丁鱼就聚集在河口找食吃。"

> **注意** 说话者在中间的时候,可以将其调整到前面翻译;started翻译为具体化"修建……之前";the mouth of the river表示"河口"。

Now there is no mud, and no food for the fish——they've left us.
现在泥沙没有了,鱼没有可吃的了,也就不来了。

> **注意** 中文为有灵主语句,英文为无灵主语句,所以no food这句就换主语为the fish;破折号后面主语出现两次可以省略。

"If all this can happen in 25 years, what will happen after 50 years, or 100 or 200?" asked Muhammad.
"如果说二十五年就发生这么多变化,五十年、一百年、二百年之后又会怎么样呢?"穆罕默德问道。

> **注意** all指上文中的"变化";后面的主谓倒置,翻译时要用正常语序。

Adelaide 阿德莱德

本文选自《简明大不列颠百科全书》第一卷,主要介绍了澳大利亚重要城市——阿德莱德的主要情况。本文属于非文学翻译,译者不详,但是百科全书的翻译有其独特的方式,特别是数字的翻译要引起重视。

Unit 3 Geography

Adelaide, capital of the state of South Australia.

阿德莱德是澳大利亚南澳大利亚州首府。

 同位语采取主谓翻译的方法。

Situated at the base of the Mt. Lofty Ranges, 9 mi (14km) inland from the centre of the east shore of the Gulf St. Vincent, it enjoys a Mediterranean climate with hot summers (February mean temperature 74°F [23°C]), cool winters (July mean 54°C [12°C]), and an average annual rainfall of 21 in (530mm).

阿德莱德位于洛夫蒂岭山麓，距圣文森特湾东岸的中心有14公里，属地中海型气候。夏季炎热，（二月份平均温度是23℃），冬季比较凉爽，（七月份平均气温是12℃），平均的年降水量是530毫米。

注意 分词位于句首找主语；enjoys不能翻译为"享受"，需翻译为"属于"；hot summers偏正短语主谓译法，后面词组翻译方法同样。

The site, chosen (1836) by Charles Sturt and William Light (the colony's first surveyor general), is on slightly rising ground along the Torrens River, which divides it into a southern business district and a northern residential section.

该城建于托伦斯沿岸的略高处，这一地点是查尔斯·斯塔特和威廉·莱特（本殖民区的第一任测量总监）于1836年选定的。托伦斯河把阿德莱德分成两个区，河南部为商业区，河北部为住宅区。

> **注意** 中间插入语过长，所以放在句子之外形成主谓结构；非限定性定语从句采用后置译法；divides的翻译很巧妙；it具体化为"阿德莱德"。

The city is separated from its suburbs by extensive areas of park lands.

市区和郊区之间有大片的公园区。

> **注意** 这个句子的亮点是is separated from的翻译，不翻译成被动语态，翻译得巧妙。

Named for Queen Adelaide, consort of the British King William IV, it was incorporated as Australia's first municipal government in 1840 and became a city in 1919, when it gained a lord mayoralty.

该城是以英王威廉四世之王后阿德莱德的名字命名的。1840年阿德莱德成立澳大利亚第一个地方自治政府，1919年设立市长职位，改为市。

> **注意** 分词位于句首，先找主语再进行翻译；主句中被动语态采用"有被不用被"的译法。

The fertility of the surrounding plains, easy access to the Murray lowlands to the east and southeast, and the presence of mineral deposits in the nearby hills all contributed to the city's growth.

四周平原土壤肥沃，与在东方和东南方的墨累低地相通，附近山区有矿藏，所有的这些都有助于城市的发展。

Unit 3　Geography　　53

> **注意** 主语较长,单独翻译;而且两个主语都用到了偏正短语的主谓译法。

As an early agricultural marketing centre, it handled wheat, wool, fruits, and wine.

阿德莱德作为早期的农贸中心,交易麦子、毛纺制品、水果以及酒类。

> **注意** 中文先说主语,再说辅助语,最后说主要内容,英文先说主语,再说主要内容,辅助语位置一般处于句首或是句末。

Adelaide, aided by its central position and a ready supply of raw materials, has since become industrialized, with factories producing automobile components, machinery, textiles, and chemicals.

从这以后,阿德莱德拥有中心的位置以及丰富的原材料,现已工业化。工厂可以生产汽车部件、机器、纺织品和化工品。

> **注意** since提到了句首,翻译为"从这以后";分词较长,可以当做从句翻译;with的独立主格结构可以翻译为主谓结构。

A focus of rail, sea, air, and road transportation, it receives the bulk of the products of the lower Murray River Valley, which has no port at its mouth.

阿德莱德是铁路、海运、空运以及公路运输的中心,接收了较低的墨累河河谷的大部分产品,因为墨累河谷地带在河口处没有港口。

> **注意** 句首的同位语需要主语，所以增主语"阿德莱德"；the bulk of 表示"大部分"，是固定用法，有一年考研英语的完形填空考过；最后的非限定性定语从句采取了后置的译法。

Adelaide's own harbour facilities are at Port Adelaide (q.v.), 7 mi (11km) northwest.

阿德莱德自己港口的设施位于它西北角11公里远的阿德莱德港。

> **注意** q.v.是拉丁语quod vide的缩写，意思是"参看该条"，这是词典里的一个常用术语。

Notable city landmarks include the university (founded in 1874), Parliament and Government houses, the Natural History Museum, and two cathedrals——St. Peter's (Anglican) and St. Francis Xavier's (Roman Catholic).

著名的城市地标包括建于1874年的大学、议会以及政府官邸、自然历史博物馆、英国圣公会圣彼得大教堂和罗马天主教圣弗朗西斯·查威尔大教堂。

> **注意** 句子结构工整，可以直接翻译；Anglican表示"圣公会"。

The Adelaide Festival of Arts (1960) was the first international celebration of its kind to be held in Australia.

1960年阿德莱德文艺节是在澳大利亚举办的第一个国际性文艺活动。

Unit 3　Geography　　55

注意 不定式 to be held 的翻译方法。

Pop. (1975 est.) city, 15,000; metropolitan area, 899,300.

人口：市1.5万（1975年估算）；都市区899，300。

注意 Pop.缩写表示"人口"；metropolitan area表示"都市区"。

The Imperial palace（Excerpt）　故宫（节选）

本文选自于The Official Guidebook of China，原本应该是汉译英的文章。在庄绎传的书中并没有给出参考译文，在本书中，作者尝试翻译，并给出了每句的详尽解释。本文属于典型的非文学翻译，注意中国特色词汇的翻译。

Built in the early fifteenth century (1406-1420 A.D.), it is also called the Palace Museum or the Old Palace.

故宫建于十五世纪早期（公元1406-1420年），也称为故宫博物院或故宫。

注意 分词位于句首找主语，先翻译主语；主语出现第二次可以不翻译。

As you pass through Tian An Men Gate you will enter a walled courtyard.

穿过天安门以后，你就进入了一个有墙的庭院。

> **注意** 短句需要断句；walled是一个形容词，可以理解为"有墙的"。

Although you cannot see them, on either side of this courtyard are many gardens and halls.

你尽管看不到，但是，在这个庭院的两边有很多的花园和大厅。

> **注意** 先说主语；either应当翻译为"两边"，中文强调整体，英文强调个体。

Of particular interest if you have time might be the Imperial Ancestral Temple, which is to the right, and the Sun Yat-Sen Park, on the left.

你如果有时间，右边的太庙和左边的中山公园都非常值得一看。

> **注意** if you have time属于插入语，表示观点，可以放在句首翻译；后面的地点状语较长，所以可以倒置结构进行翻译；Of particular interest表示"有特别地兴趣"，可以处理为"非常值得一看"。

Covering an area of 175 acres (72 ha.), the Palace is enclosed by walls over 35ft. (10.4 m.) high and surrounded by a moat 57 yd. (52 m.) wide.

故宫占地面积72公顷，围墙10.4米高，护城河有52米宽。

Unit 3 Geography   57

> **注意** 分词位于句首，先找主语；后面的被动语态直接省略，处理得很巧妙；所有的量词都翻译为中文中有的量词，英文中的可以省略。

Today this moat is still full of water.
直到现在，护城河还是注满了水。

> **注意** 再短的句子也要断句；be full of 翻译为"注满"比较好。

Four watchtowers are placed, one at each corner.
四周各有一个角楼。

> **注意** 这个句子中的 watchtowers 翻译为中国特色的"角楼"；后面小分句可以放在句子中进行合译。

Used as the imperial palace by both the Ming and Qing Dynasties (1368-1911 A.D.), the Imperial Palace is the largest and most complete group of ancient buildings standing in China.
故宫作为明、清两代的皇宫（公元1368-1911年），是中国现存的最大的、也是最完整的古建筑群。

> **注意** 分词位于句首，先找主语；standing 可以翻译为"现存的"；句中几个专有名词翻译时要注意。

The halls and palaces which comprise the Imperial Palace are all built of wood and brick.
构成故宫的宫和殿都是由木材和砖块建成的。

定语从句较短,可以采用前置译法;被动语态用了"有被不用被"的译法。

With a total of over nine thousand rooms, most of the Palace had undergone some reconstruction to repair damage caused by fire and other ravages of time during the long years of its history.

故宫共有九千多间房子,大部分都进行了重建,来修复在漫长历史当中由火灾或者时间流逝带来的破坏。

 状语在句首,所以需要找到主语,先说主语;to表示目的,需要断句;its属于物主代词,可以不翻译。

Throughout you will find typical masterpieces of ancient Chinese architecture.

从头到尾你都会发现中国古代建筑师们留下的杰作。

 ancient Chinese architecture翻译为"中国古代建筑师们",而不是"中国古代建筑"。

Two notable examples are the ingeniously constructed watchtowers and the magnificent Hall of Supreme Harmony.

建筑巧妙的角楼以及庄严宏伟的太和殿是其中最值得一提的两个例子。

 ingeniously constructed和magnificent两个词组可以翻译为四字短语,形成对应结构;太和殿的英文说法很重要。

Unit 3　Geography

To further insure the Imperial Palace would be given special protection, in 1961 the Chinese government decreed that the entire area be considered one of China's "most important historical sites".

为了进一步确保故宫受到特别的保护，中国政府于1961年颁布条令，规定将整个故宫地区划为中国最重要的历史遗迹。

 前面的被动语态翻译为"受到"；主句中宾语从句翻译为同位语从句；宾语从句中的虚拟语气也值得注意。

The Palace Museum, with four gates, has its main entrance to the south, known as the Meridian Gate.

故宫博物院共有四个大门，它的主门是南门，也叫午门。

 前面with结构翻译为主谓结构；后面"午门"的翻译亦要注意。

This is the gate you will approach as you continue along the cobbled roadway from Tian An Men.

沿着天安门的那条石子路向前就能走到午门。

 cobbled翻译为"石子"；the gate指的就是前文的"午门"。

The Imperial Palace is divided into two ceremonial areas: the Outer Palace and the Inner Court.

故宫博物院分为两个重要的区域，一是外朝，二是内廷。

 前面的被动语态采用"有被不用被"的译法；后面两个名词的翻译要注意。

Through the Meridian Gate and across the Golden Water Bridge, one comes to the Gate of Supreme Harmony, the main gate of the Outer Palace.

穿过午门,跨过金水桥,我们就来到了太和门,这是外朝的主门。

> **注意** 句子中介词through翻译为动词;要注意"太和门"的英文译法以及最后同位语的译法。

The main buildings in the Outer Palace are the Hall of Supreme Harmony, the Hall of Complete Harmony, and the Hall of Preserving Harmony.

太和门是外朝的主门,外朝的主要建筑是太和殿、中和殿、保和殿。

> **注意** 前面主语中的状语采用了偏正短语的主谓译法;后面三个殿的译法也很重要。

Economy

A Global Economy 一个全球性的经济

本文摘选自1995年Kantor大使在对外经济贸易大学的演讲,主要涉及全球经济问题,属于典型的非文学翻译,译者不详,翻译方法体现得较多,特别是经济类专有名词更多。

President Clinton realized——as all of us must——that today's economy is global.

正如每个人必须认识到的那样,克林顿总统认识到当今的经济具有全球性质。

> **注意** 插入语表示观点可以提到句首翻译;today翻译为"当今",而不是"今天";global可以认为是抽象形容词,翻译时增词。

We live in an era in which information, goods and capital speed around the globe, every hour of every day.

我们生活在这样一个时代中,信息、货物和资金每时每刻在世界上流动。

定语从句较长,翻译时进行后置;最后的状语可以提到句中翻译。

Whether we like it or not, all of our fortunes are tied together. We are truly interdependent.

我们不管喜欢与否,我们所有的命运都是相连的,我们真的需要相互依存。

 先说主语;句子较短可以和后面句子合译;interdependent 翻译为"相互依存"。

America supports international trade because we believe fundamentally that trade will enrich those nations who embrace its discipline.

美国支持国际贸易,因为我们确信,贸易会让遵守行为准则的国家富裕起来。

 断句的点在什么地方;those who 不要翻译为"那些国家"。

The great promise of trade is its potential to promote mutual prosperity——and to strengthen the bonds between sovereign nations.

极其光明的贸易前景是促进相互繁荣和加强主权国家之间联系的潜在力量。

 promise 相当于 basis for expectation;注意"相互繁荣"和"主权国家"的译法。

Unit 4　Economy　　63

The U.S. and China both demonstrate the potential of trade to improve the lives of our people.

美中两国都显示一种能提高两国人民生活的贸易潜力。

注意　the U.S. and China翻译为同位结构；to后面的结构是前面词组的定语。

You know better than I the great achievements of the Chinese economy over the past two decades.

你们比我更清楚中国经济在过去二十年中所取得的伟大成就。

注意　achievements属于典型的抽象名词，所以需要增词翻译。

In 1977, the sum total of Chinese imports and exports was less than $15 billion, putting China's share of world trade at 0.6 percent.

在1977年，中国进出口总额还不到150亿美元，仅占世界贸易总额的0.6%。

注意　这句话的重点是数字翻译；数字翻译亦是笔译的重点。

The most populous country in the world, China ranked a distant 30th among exporting nations.

中国是世界上人口最多的国家，在出口国家中排名靠后，仅在第30位。

注意　句首同位语可以用主谓译法；后面句子中的数字放在最后翻译，这样会比较通顺。

By 1993 China's exports and imports totaled nearly $ 200 billion.
到1993年，中国进出口总额接近2000亿美元。

 by表示"到"；total可以表示"总额达到"；数字翻译很重要。

China had become the world's tenth largest exporter.
中国已成为第十大出口国。

 这句话当中的过去完成时和上句话有一定关系，可以直接翻译。

Since 1978, when China began opening its economy to increased foreign investment and trade, aggregate output has more than doubled.
自从1978年以来，中国经济为日益增加的外国投资和贸易敞开大门，总产量增加了一倍多。

 这句话主句中换主语的译法非常重要，将原主语China换为了"中国经济"，这是主谓的偏正译法；后面的more than doubled翻译为"增加了"，这和"增加到"有一定差异。

The strongest growth has occurred in the coastal areas near Hong Kong and opposite Taiwan, where foreign investment and modern production methods have spurred production of both domestic and export goods.
最强劲的增长发生在靠近香港和台湾对面的沿海地区，在那里，外国投资和现代生产手段的使用促进了国内和出口货物的生产。

where做后置定语翻译时，翻译为"在那里"；"手段"后面的增词比较难，也可以不增词；"国内外"如何翻译。

Per capita GNP has grown at an average rate of 7.6% from 1980 to 1992.

从1980年至1992年，人均国民生产总值平均增长率为7.6%。

 "人均"如何翻译；"国民生产总值"如何翻译。

The numbers are interesting, but how has this affected the people of China?

看看数字是很有趣的。然而这又是怎样影响中国人的呢？

 这个句子翻译得很有意思，为了通顺，增动词"看看"。

In the last decade, telephone connections rose more than 60%.

在过去十年中，电话用户增加了60%以上。

 decade的用法；电话用户如何翻译。

Electrical production more than doubled to 621 million kilowatt hours.

电力生产增加了一倍多，达到6.21亿千瓦小时。

 短句子中间的断句；后面的kilowatt hours如何翻译。

In short, China has improved the economic well-being of its people.
总之，中国提高了人民的生活水平。

"生活水平"该如何翻译，这当然是比较美国化的说法，和政府工作报告有一定区别，但是都是正确的；后面的物主代词不翻译。

The people of the United States also have experienced the benefits of world trade.
美国人民也有得益于国际贸易的经历。

这句话谓语的翻译。

Since World War II, the U.S. has been the world's largest economy and, in most years, the world's largest exporter.
自从第二次世界大战以来，美国一直是世界上最大的经济大国，在大多数年代中，它又是世界上最大的出口国。

economy翻译为"经济大国"；后面同位语采用了主谓的翻译方法。

But the importance of trade in our economy has exploded in the past three decades.
但在过去三十年中，我们经济贸易的重要性大大地增加了。

句中谓语exploded的翻译，这个词很重要，在口译中经常使用。

In 1970, the value of two way trade was equal to just 13% of the U.S. economy.

在1970年,双向贸易的总值占了整个美国经济的13%。

 "双向贸易"和"双边贸易"翻译是不一样的;"占"这个词的翻译也很重要,口译中经常使用。

Last year, that figure, at 28%, was more than twice as high.

去年这一数字上升到28%,比1970年增加了一倍多。

 at表示"到",more than twice表示"增加了一倍多"。

In just the last seven years, jobs supported by U.S. exports (goods and services) have risen by 4 million, to a total of 11 million.

就在过去七年中,美国的出口(货物和服务)创造的就业机会增加了400万个,总数上升到1100万个。

 分词位于名词后,相当于定语从句。

That's almost one out of ten American jobs.

这个数字就占美国就业总数的1/10。

 that翻译为"这";分数的表达法。

Last year U.S. trade equaled $1.8 trillion.

去年,美国贸易总额达到了1.8万亿美元。

 "总额达到"用动词equal;"万亿"用trillion。

Nor is the importance of trade likely to diminish for either China or the United States.

无论是中国还是美国，都不会缩小贸易的重要性。

 这句话是部分倒装的形式；而且在翻译时需要换主语。

China will continue to depend upon lucrative export markets to earn the foreign exchange it needs to develop and grow.

中国会继续依靠获利的出口市场，来赚取外汇以发展和增长自己的经济。

 这句话的断句；lucrative表示"有利可图的"；最后的定语从句翻译为状语从句，这表示定语和状语的互换。

At the same time, China's imports will supply the much needed machinery and technology to fuel its continued development.

同时，中国可以用进口的机械和技术来加速它继续发展的速度。

 句子换主语的情况，偏正短语取偏做主语；fuel翻译为"加速"。

For the United States, new commercial opportunities will grow most rapidly in the emerging markets.

对于美国来说，在不断涌现的市场上，新的贸易机会将以最快的速度增加。

 for位于句首翻译为"对于"；"速度"为范畴词，这是增词的现象。

We estimate that three quarters of new export opportunities over the next twenty years——that's an incredible $1.9 trillion in potential exports——will come in the emerging markets of Asia and Latin America.

我们估计过，在未来的二十年中，新的出口机会中的3/4，即数量可观的1.9万亿美元的潜在出口额，将来自亚洲和拉丁美洲不断出现的市场上。

 本句需要断句；中间的插入语不改变位置直接翻译。

This means jobs for American workers and a higher standard of living for the American people.

这将意味着为美国工人创造就业机会，让美国人民提高生活水平。

 抽象名词jobs可以增词；注意后面并列结构的翻译。

China and Britain in the World Economy (Excerpt)
中国与英国在世界经济中的作用（摘录）

本文摘录于1996年英国外交部Hon Malcolm Rifkind在对外经济贸易大学的讲话，主要涉及英国和中国与世界经济的关系，属于典型的非文学翻译，但是专有名词较多，需要记忆。

Britain and the World Economy
英国与世界经济

My theme today is the world economy.
我今天演讲的主题是世界经济。

句中增词"演讲",不增加亦可。

The future of the world economy is of particular interest to my country because we have such a huge stake in it.

世界经济的未来与我国休戚相关,所以我们格外关注。

 先说主语,再说辅助语;stake的用法很重要;of particular interest如何理解更加重要。

Britain lives by commerce.

英国的生存依赖贸易。

 换主语,主谓结构的偏正译法。

With 2% of the world's population, we are the world's fifth largest trading nation.

英国人口虽然只占全球的2%,它却是世界第五大贸易国。

 先说主语;两个分句之间的关系如何翻译;"贸易国"如何翻译。

We rely more than any other major economy on the goods and services that we export, the investment that we attract and we make abroad.

我们对商品和服务出口以及对投资和引资的依赖,超过了世界上其他主要经济体。

Unit 4 Economy 71

> **注意** 先摆事实，后评论；the investment that we attract and we make abroad翻译为"投资和引资"。

The strength of our financial services sector is well-known; the world's leading centre for international bank lending, foreign exchange, aviation and marine insurance, for example.

我们的金融服务业以实力雄厚而著称，我们是国际银行借贷、外汇以及航空和海事保险业的中心。

> **注意** 分号后面的同位语用主谓翻译；international bank lending翻译为"国际银行借贷"；marine insurance翻译为"海事保险"。

But British exports range far beyond services, important as they are.

服务业尽管在英国的出口中占重要地位，但英国的出口绝不仅限于服务业。

> **注意** as做让步从句的引导词，且引起倒装；they的指代很重要；主句中有主谓的偏正译法。

We export one quarter of all we produce; more per head than either Japan or the United States.

我们四分之一的产品供出口，人均出口量高于美国和日本。

> **注意** 主句主谓结构采用偏正译法；定语从句的译法很巧妙。

Our place in the flows of global capital is equally central.

我们在全球资本流动方面也居中心地位。

 the flows of global capital翻译为"全球资本流动"；可以增词"方面"。

27% of all foreign exchange dealing takes place in London.
全球外汇交易的27%在伦敦进行。

 foreign exchange dealing翻译为"全球外汇交易"。

Britain is the world's third largest outward investor.
英国是世界上第三大对外投资者。

 outward如何翻译。

We ourselves attract more foreign investment than any country but the U.S.; more U.S. investment than in the whole Pacific region.
同时我们所吸引的外资额仅次于美国，居世界第二，而美国在英投资高于其在整个太平洋地区的投资总和。

 than any country but the U.S.是如何处理的；后面的more than结构如何翻译。

The fruits of this two-way flow are substantial.
这种双向资金流动让我们受益颇丰。

 主语中fruits的翻译；而且增加对象词"让我们"。

Unit 4　Economy

Our overseas investments yield Britain a net income of over £10 billion a year.

每年英国的海外投资为我们带来超过100亿英镑的净收入。

 yield的翻译；"净收入"如何翻译；"英镑"的写法。

In the last five years inward investment in Britain has brought our people more than 250,000 new jobs.

而过去五年，外国对英投资为我国人民创造了25万个就业机会。

 句子的断句；jobs翻译为"就业机会"。

What this means is that Britain has direct experience of the benefits that international trade and investment generate.

这意味着英国直接享受到了国际投资所带来的利益。

主语从句的翻译；定语从句较短，采用前置译法；benefits 属于抽象名词，运用增词的译法。

We have a major interest in seeing it flourish.

国际投资的蓬勃发展符合我国利益。

 这句话属于意译，为了让句子更加通顺，把前后的主谓颠倒翻译。

We have a major interest in creating the right climate for that to happen.

我们非常愿意为此创造一个良好的环境。

 climate翻译为"环境"或是"氛围",这个词很重要,如"学习风气"应当翻译为learning climate,在某年的考研完形填空中曾经出现过。

China in the World Economy
世界经济中的中国

What is China's expanding role in this?

在世界经济中,中国将在哪些方面发挥日益重要的作用呢?

 上下文的增词。

China's vast size and resources, her extraordinary economic progress over recent years, have made her an increasingly important player in the modern international economy.

中国地大物博,近年来经济迅猛发展,这让中国在现代国际经济中成为一支越来越重要的力量。

 主语偏正短语,采用主谓译法;外位语与本位词的译法;代词her的翻译。

Because of this, because of Britain's own huge stake in the world economy, we need to take a real interest in China.

中国在现代国际经济中的地位,以及我国在世界经济中的巨大利益,这一切让我们需要密切关注中国。

> **注意** this指的是上文的句子,需要仔细查看一下;后面"这一切"为本位词的译法。

Since economic reform began in 1978, an average growth rate of almost 10% a year has seen China's GNP nearly quadruple.

自1978年经济改革以来,中国经济以年均近10%的速度增长,让其国民生产总值几乎翻了两番。

> **注意** "年均增长率"如何翻译,这是口译考试的重点词组;quadruple可以翻译为"翻两番","增长了三倍","增长到四倍","二、三、四"都用上,中文十分准确。

The rewards for the people of China are clear, most visibly in the dynamism and prosperity of Peking and the coastal cities.

中国人民获得的实惠有目共睹,北京和沿海城市的繁荣和盎然生机便是最明显的见证。

> **注意** rewards为典型的抽象名词;后面句子中的dynamism and prosperity也属于抽象名词,翻译得比较复杂;visibly改变词性。

For the international community the most striking consequence of these changes is that China has grown to be the world's eleventh largest economy, and is set to grow further.

对国际社会来说,这些变化带来的最引人注目的结果是,中国已跃居为世界第十一大经济体,而且今后定会发展更快。

for 位于句首,翻译为"对于";consequence 为典型的抽象名词,翻译时需要增词。

China's rapid emergence as a major world actor is a tribute to the drive and entrepreneurial spirit of her people, and more particularly to the fundamental economic reforms she has pursued over the past two decades.

中国迅速崛起,成为世界上发挥重大作用的国家,这应当归功于中国人民的努力和进取精神,尤其是过去二十年里中国所进行的根本性的经济改革。

 主语偏正短语,采用主谓译法;本位词与外位语的关系;后面句子定语从句前置;本句词汇较难。

It is a clear testimony to the success of the open door policy led by Mr. Deng Xiaoping.

这无疑证明了邓小平先生倡导的开放政策是成功的。

注意 testimony 词性转换;success 是典型的抽象名词,注意其翻译方法;the open door policy 用法比较少见,有感情色彩。

I warmly welcome those reforms and that success.

我对这些改革及其成功表示热烈欢迎。

注意 事实与评论的关系,中文先摆事实再评论,英文先评论后摆事实。

Unit 4　Economy　77

I would draw a further conclusion, which I believe is central to assessing China's future place in the world economy.

我还有一个想法，我认为我的这一想法对于估价中国今后在世界经济中的地位是至关重要的。

 非限定性定语从句的翻译方法；I believe是插入语，表示观点，可以采用前置译法；central to表示"至关重要"。

In my view China's growing international engagement has been vital to her progress.

我认为，中国日益扩大的国际接触对其进步一直是至关重要的。

 engagement的翻译很重要；her的翻译亦很重要。

The key to sustaining and building on early economic success was China's move into world markets.

中国能够在已取得的经济成功的基础上进一步发展，关键是它进入了世界市场。

 这句话十分难以理解，它属于主语和宾语（表语）的修饰成分互换，属于高级笔译的范畴，而且要注意上下文的关系。

Consider a couple of statistics.

让我们看几个统计数字。

 为了上下文的通顺，这句话需要增词；statistics增范畴词"数字"。

Since 1979 foreign trade as a share of China's GNP has risen from 10% to 45%.

1979年以来，外贸占中国国民生产总值的比重从10%上升到45%。

 短句需要断句；China's GNP如何翻译。

Integration in world markets became a basic fact of Chinese economic life.

融入世界市场已成为中国经济生活的一个基本事实。

 句子主谓宾工整，只要把基本词汇翻译正确即可。

With that came integration into the world investment system.

继之而来的是融入世界投资体系。

 句中的抽象名词integration，应该翻译为动词"融入"。

Foreign funds flowed into China in a spectacular way.

外国资金大量流入中国。

 funds可以表示"资金"；in a spectacular way表示"可观地，大量地"。

The stock of foreign investment grew from under $ 5 billion in 1989 to nearly $ 90 billion by 1994.

外资存量是从1989年的不足50亿美元上升到1994年的近900亿美元。

Unit 4　Economy　79

注意 the stock of foreign investment表示"外资存量";数字表达法很重要。

So China has built new and increasingly strong links, in both directions, with world markets.

总之,中国与世界市场之间建立起了双向的、新的联系,这些联系正在日益加强。

注意 中文先说主语,再说辅助语;increasingly strong属于较长的形容词和副词,可以单独成句。

These links have contributed to creation of new jobs, new prosperity for China. What next?

这些联系为中国创造了新的就业机会,带来了新的繁荣。那么今后怎么办呢?

 注意 creation和prosperity属于抽象名词,需要增词或是改变词性。

I believe it is China's interest to build on this foundation, to consolidate her place in the international system.

我相信,在此基础上进一步努力并巩固中国在国际体系中的地位符合中国的利益。

 注意 本句需要断句;it为形式主语,翻译时应当最先翻译。

That is the way to maximize her share of world markets; and ——as the U.K. knows from direct experience——to attract the stimulus, the technology and the funding that inward investment can offer.

这也是最大限度地扩大其在世界市场份额的方法。英国从自身直接的经历中体会到，吸引外资可以带来动力、技术和资金。

分号表示句号；knows意译为"体会到"；that inward investment can offer可以直接不翻译，比较简单。

中国能依靠自己的力量实现粮食基本自给

China Can Basically Achieve Self-Sufficiency in Grain through Self-Reliance

本文选自于《北京周报》中《中国的粮食问题》第三部分，属于重大的农业经济问题，译者不详。本文是典型的非文学翻译，句式工整，但是词汇较难，注意记忆。

立足国内资源，实现粮食基本自给，是中国解决粮食供需问题的基本方针。

The basic principle for solving the problem of grain supply and demand in China is to rely on the domestic resources and basically achieve self-sufficiency in grain.

本句主语较长，可以先翻译句子后部的表语；时态的表达很重要；连词选择很重要；专业词组表达很重要。

中国将努力促进国内粮食增产，在正常情况下，粮食自给率不低于95%，净进口量不超过国内消费量的5%。

Unit 4　Economy

China endeavors to increase its grain production so that its self-sufficiency rate of grain under normal conditions will be above 95 percent and the net import rate 5 percent, or even less, of the total consumption quantity.

> **注意**　"努力促进"副词+动词可以翻译为谓语动词过渡；连词的使用十分重要；专业词组表达很重要。

现阶段中国已经实现了粮食基本自给，在未来的发展过程中，中国依靠自己的力量实现粮食基本自给，客观上具备诸多有利因素。根据中国农业自然资源、生产条件、技术水平和其他发展条件，粮食增产潜力很大。

China has basically achieved self-sufficiency in grain at the present stage, and there are many favorable objective factors for her to maintain such achievement by her own efforts in the course of future development: Natural agricultural resources, production conditions, technical level and some other conditions ensure great potential in this respect.

> **注意**　这是一个典型的中文两句合译的句子；"根据"后面的内容就是"有利因素"，所以可以合译；"中国农业自然资源、生产条件、技术水平和其他发展条件"可以让"粮食增产"；注意专有名词的使用。

一是提高现有耕地单位面积产量有潜力。

There is potential for increasing the yield per unit area on the existing cultivated land.

> **注意**　"有潜力"表示评论，前面是事实；"单位面积产量"是典型的口译词汇。

目前，中国同一类型地区粮食单产水平悬殊，高的每公顷7500—15000公斤，低的只有3000—5000公斤。

At present, the per unit area yield of grain varies widely in the same districts, the highest yield being 7,500kg to 15,000kg per hectare, and the lowest 3,000kg to 5,000kg.

"水平"为范畴词，可以省略不译；后面用了分词的独立主格结构。

在播种面积相对稳定的前提下，只要1996—2010年粮食单产年均递增1%，2011—2030年年均递增0.7%，就可以达到预期的粮食总产量目标。

Given a relatively stable sown area, China can achieve its desired total grain output target if the annual average increase rate of per unit area yield is one percent from 1996 to 2010 and 0.7 percent from 2011 to 2030.

条件句中有范畴词"前提"；最后一个分句前缺少主语，所以可以增主语"中国"；"粮食单产"和"年均递增"都是口笔译考试的重要词组，需要记住。

这样的速度与过去46年年均递增3.1%相比，是比较低的。

Compared to the annual average increase rate of 3.1 percent of the per unit area yield in the past 46 years, it is clear that one percent and 0.7 percent are fairly low.

"与……相比"是固定词组；"比较"不是比较级，而是原级；而且注意增加比较的对象词。

即使考虑到土地报酬率递减的因素，也是有条件实现的。

So, to achieve the target is totally possible even if the factor of diminishing land returns rate is considered.

> **注意** "考虑到……"是无主语句，所以可以用被动语态的翻译方法；后面句子强调"有条件"。

目前，中国粮食单产水平与世界粮食高产国家相比也是比较低的，中国要在短时间内达到粮食高产国家的水平难度较大，但是经过努力是完全可以缩小差距的。

At present, China's per unit area yield of grain is low compared with countries with high grain yields. It will be difficult for China to reach the level of countries with high grain production in a short period of time, but the gap can certainly be narrowed through earnest efforts.

> **注意** 中文句子较长是可以分译的；"比较低"不是比较级，而是原级；"难度较大"属于评论性词，所以可以放在句首翻译；最后一个句子缺少主语，可以增主语。

通过改革中低产田、兴修水利、扩大灌溉面积、推广先进适用技术等工程和生物措施，可使每公顷产量提高1500公斤以上。

The grain output per hectare can be increased by more than 1,500 kg through the upgrading of medium-and-low-yield land, intensifying water-control projects, enlarging irrigated areas and spreading the use of advanced agrotechnology.

> **注意** 前后条件和结果的关系，先翻译结果，再翻译条件；中文里的动词可以翻译为抽象名词；"等工程和生物措施"应该属于翻

> 译时的漏译，没有原因，只是翻译时可能没有注意。

二是开发后备耕地资源有潜力。

There is also potential for exploiting untouched arable land resources.

> **注意** "有潜力"是评论，可以放在前面翻译；"耕地"翻译为 arable land。

中国现有宜农荒地3500万公顷，其中可开垦为耕地的约有1470万公顷。

China now has 35 million hectares of wasteland which are suitable for farming, including about 14.7 million hectares can be reclaimed.

> **注意** "宜农荒地"的翻译方法；"可"这个汉字可以表示被动语态。

中国政府将在加强对现有耕地保护的同时，加快宜农荒地的开发和工矿废弃地的复垦。

The Chinese government will make efforts to speed up the reclamation of wasteland suitable for farming as well as land discarded by factories and mines, while measures will be adopted to protect the existing cultivated land.

> **注意** 本句需要了解主句和从句的关系，注意先翻译谁，再翻译谁；而且主语和谓语的关系需要辨别。

未来几十年计划每年开发复垦30万公顷以上,以弥补同期耕地占用,保持耕地面积长期稳定。

In the next few decades China plans to reclaim more than 300,000 hectares each year to make up for the loss of cultivated land appropriated for non-farming uses and to keep the area of cultivated land constant for a long period of time.

注意 本句需要增加主语;"以"表示目的,翻译为to;专有名词翻译需要注意。

通过提高复种指数,使粮食作物播种面积稳定在1.1亿公顷左右。

The grain-sown area will be stabilized at about 110 million hectares through the increase of the multiple crop index.

注意 主句没有主语,可以用被动语态;the increase of是抽象名词的翻译方法。

Unit 5 *Culture*

A Valentine to One Who Cared——Too Much
衷肠曲

本文作者是美国人南希·J·里格，选自于Los Angeles Times，属于典型的文学作品，特别是对于景物和心理的描写居多，所以在翻译时需要体现词汇的用法，很多地方用到意译的翻译方法。

It's raining, again.
又下雨了。

 注意 本句无难点，但是注意again的使用，文学色彩较浓。

As I lie awake in bed, listening to the sound of those razor-sharp drops pounding on the pavement, my mind goes reeling down dark corridors teeming with agonizing flashbacks, and a chill from within fills me with dread.

我躺在床上，睡不着，听着雨点儿落在路面上啪啪作响。我思绪万千，恍恍惚惚进入了一条条幽暗的通道，回想起许多痛苦的往事，心里一阵冰凉，不禁感到毛骨悚然。

 awake可以单独翻译；agonizing可以单独翻译；with dread 用成语翻译，文学色彩较浓。

It does this every year in Southern California; at least that's what they told me last year when I marveled at the relentless determination of the rain.

加利福尼亚南部，年年如此；去年，雨无情地下个不停，我表示惊异，人们就是这样对我说的。

 when引导从句的翻译位置；relentless的翻译需要注意。

There seem to be two seasons here.
这里似乎只有两个季节。

 本句无难点，直接翻译。

During the rainy season, sometimes the storms drench the area nonstop for days.

在雨季，狂风暴雨有时一连几天不停。

 这句当中"有时"的翻译是亮点，译者在翻译时将同一句中的词进行了拆分。

Sometimes the storm come and go.
有时一会儿就雨过天晴。

 这句可以和上一句连接翻译，come and go表示瞬间过去，所以可以翻译为"雨过天晴"。

Often property damage and disrupted lives result.

结果往往是财产遭损失,生活受影响。

 再短的句子也需要断句;disrupted lives result这个句子的翻译用了意译的方法。

It's hard to predict the intensity of the patterns from year to year.

严重程度如何,年年不同,难以预料。

 It's hard to predict表示评论,所以放在最后翻译。

Then there is the fire season.

再就是火季。

 fire season表示"火季"。

That takes care of the property that managed to survive the deluge, again disrupting lives.

大雨过后勉强剩下的财物就落到它的手里,人们的生活再次受到影响。

 deluge指的不是"洪水",根据上下文,而是"大雨";句子用了拟人的方法进行翻译。

The days connecting these seasons are monotonous, with some sun, some smog and some more sun.

这两个季节之间的日子是非常单调的,有时见一点儿阳光,有时烟雾弥漫,过后再见一点儿阳光。

connecting动词翻译为介词"之间",这种动词和介词的互换要注意。

This is nothing like back home in Colorado.
这跟家乡科罗拉多的情况迥然不同。

 这里用nothing来表示否定;Colorado翻译为"科罗拉多"。

We have rains there, too.
科罗拉多也下雨。

 本句很短,但是要注意代词的译法,we表示"科罗拉多",需要具体化。

Thunderstorms in spring and summer often come with intensity great enough to cause flash-flooding.
春夏两季雷雨交加,猛烈异常,往往顷刻之间暴雨成灾。

 断句的位置;intensity great翻译为小句子。

Every child raised in the West knows about these dangers.
在西部长大的孩子都知道洪水的厉害。

 这里的west指的是美国的西部;"的厉害"属于增范畴词。

At least that's what I used to think. I'm not so sure anymore.

至少我过去是这样想的，现在就不敢说了。

两个句子比较短，可以合译；uscd to表示过去常常如何。

In second grade they showed us a terrifying film about flash-flooding.

我上二年级的时候，给我们演过一场暴雨成灾的电影，非常可怕。

文学作品增词较多，范围较广，无固定模式；terrifying属于较长的形容词，可以单独翻译。

A man parked his 57 Chevy on a little bridge overlooking a picturesque, arid gully and took out his camera. It was starting to rain, but he really wanted to get that picture.

电影里有位先生把他那57型车威牌小轿车停在一座小桥上，小桥下面是条美丽、干涸的狭谷。这位先生拿出相机准备拍照，却下起雨来。可是他实在想把这里的景色拍下来再走。

"电影里"属于上下文的增词；overlooking要注意翻译时的处理。

The image of a sudden wall of dark water carrying the man and his car away in an instant is still imprinted on my mind.

突然浑浊的雨水像一面墙一样压了下来，一下子就连人带车都冲走了。这情景直到现在还印在我的脑海里。

> **注意** the image引起的主语较长，所以可以单独翻译；后面用本位词"这情景"替代前面的句子。

They used this kind of scare tactic when I was growing up. I wonder what they use today.

我小的时候，他们用过这种吓唬的办法。现在用什么办法就不得而知了。

> **注意** when I was growing表示"我小的时候"；后面句子较短，所以可以合译。

A year ago I would have sworn that children here are taught nothing about the dangerous powers of nature.

一年前，我敢说，从来没有人对这里的孩子讲讲大自然的力量有多么危险。

> **注意** 本句需要断句；would have sworn为虚拟语气，表示对过去情况的推测；are taught是被动语态，翻译为主动语态。

My fiancé, Earl Higgins, and I had recently moved to Los Angeles from Colorado.

那时我和未婚夫艾勒·希金斯刚从科罗拉多搬到洛杉矶来。

> had recently moved的时态翻译。

It was a move we had made by choice, for career purposes.

我们是为了事业，自愿搬来的。

> **注意** 这是一个强调句型，强调了move的方式是什么。

About a week and a half after we moved into an apartment in Atwater, a block from the Los Angeles River, the rains started in earnest.

搬来以后就在阿特瓦德区离洛杉矶河一个街区的地方找了一套房子住下。住了大约一个多星期，下起雨来了，而且下个不停。

> **注意** 英文句子讲究主从复合的关系，所以将重要的写在前面，不重要的写在后面，但是中文一般是按照时间顺序来进行写作的，所以在翻译时要遵循这种规律。

On Valentine's Day, I remember thinking what dismal weather it was for being in love, but after studying Earl's face I knew that the weather didn't matter much.

记得在圣瓦伦廷节那一天，我觉得这样的天气对正在相爱的人来说可太糟糕了。可是仔细一看艾勒的脸色，就知道天气不好并没有多大关系。

> **注意** Valentine's Day是西方的情人节；dismal表示评论，所以可以放在最后翻译；studying这个单词不是"学习"的意思，而是"仔细看看"，注意文学作品的用词。

At least that's what I thought. Because we were together, life was safe and secure.

至少当时我是这么想的。因为我们俩在一起，生活是安定的。

> **注意** safe and secure表示"安定"。

Unit 5　Culture

We talked of our plans to wed and start a family, once we were settled in Los Angeles, and we listened to the rain.

我们打算一旦在洛杉矶站住脚，就结婚，组织家庭。我们一面议论，一面听着外头的雨声。

 句子的时间顺序，先译什么，再译什么。

The Sunny nook footbridge connects Atwater with Griffith Park, spanning the Los Angeles River and the Golden State Freeway.

桑尼努克桥是一座只供人行的小桥，它横跨洛杉矶河和金州高速公路，联结着阿特瓦德区和格力非公园。

 主谓分割译法；中间各个专有名词的译法。

Like the freeway, the river is fenced to keep people out.

洛杉矶河和公路一样，为了行人的安全，两旁修了栏杆。

 再短的句子也要断句；先出主语再说辅助语。

During several walks to the park, Earl and I had noticed many children who ignored the fences and found holes to allow them through in order to play in the dirt in the river bed and run up and down the sloping concrete banks.

我和艾勒好几次散步到公园去，都看见许多孩子不管栏杆不栏杆，见了缺口就钻过去，在河床上的烂泥里玩，在两岸用水泥砌的斜坡上跑上跑下。

 先说主语；句中口语化的词汇很有特点。

Most of the time parents probably have no worry about their kids playing in the concrete channel, because most of the time the river is dry.

在大多数情况下，家长大概可以放心地让孩子们在两岸砌着水泥的河道里玩耍，因为大部分时间河里没有水。

time在这里表示"情况"，而不是"时间"；后面句中的谓语用了肯定译法。

Habits form, however, and, in a child's mind, most of the time becomes all of the time, and nobody gives it much thought. Then the rains come.

然而孩子们习以为常，在他们心目中，"大部分时间"变成了"全部时间"，而谁也没有仔细去想这件事。后来就下起雨来了。

转折词需要采用前置译法；中间的代词翻译需要注意。

How To Grow Old 怎样才能活的老

本文的作者是英国二十世纪著名的哲学家、数学家、逻辑学家和历史学家——伯纳德·罗素，他是无神论和不可知论者，也是二十世纪西方最著名、影响最大的学者和和平主义社会活动家之一。罗素也被认为与弗雷格、维特根斯坦和怀特海一同创建了分析哲学。他与怀特海合著的《数学原理》对逻辑学、数学、集合论、语言学和分析哲学有着巨大影响。1950年，罗素获得诺贝尔文学奖，以表彰其"多样且重要的作品，持续不断地追求人道主义理想和思想自由"。本文并不是其最著名的《西方哲学史》中的内容，而是选自《记忆中的肖像及其他》一书。这本书主要以散文居多，但还是属于偏文学作品的内容，翻译时略带有口语化的特点，由庄绎传翻译。

In spite of the title, this article will really be on how not to grow old, which, at my time of life, is a much more important subject.

题目虽然这样写，实际上本文所要谈的却是人怎样才可以不老。对于像我这样年纪的人来说，这个问题就更是重要得多了。

句子中究竟对how to grow old是如何理解的；subject表示"问题"。

My first advice would be to choose your ancestors carefully.

我的头一条忠告是，你可得要挑选好你的先人啊。

ancestors表示"祖先、先人"；句子翻译得比较口语化。

Although both my parents died young, I have done well in this respect as regards my other ancestors.

我的父母年纪轻轻就去世了，可是说到祖辈，我还是选得不错的。

although的转折翻译在句子的后面；as regards表示"涉及到"。

My maternal grandfather, it is true, was cut off in the flower of his youth at the age of sixty-seven, but my other three grandparents all lived to be over eighty.

我外祖父固然是在风华正茂之年就去世了，当时他只有六十七岁，但是我的祖父、祖母和外祖母却都活到了八十岁以上。

"外祖父"如何翻译;"风华正茂"如何翻译;"我的祖父、祖母和外祖母"该如何翻译。

Of remoter ancestors I can only discover one who did not live to a great age, and he died of a disease which is now rare, namely, having his head cut off.

再往远一点说,在我的先人之中,我发现只有一位活得不长,他得了一种现在已不多见的病,那就是头让人砍掉了。

 定语从句的翻译;罗素的语言诙谐幽默,在翻译时也要遵从他的语言特点。

A great-grandmother of mine, who was a friend of Gibbon, lived to the age of ninety-two, and to her last day remained a terror to all her descendants.

我的一位曾祖母,和吉本是朋友,活到了九十二岁,她直到临终都使儿孙望而生畏。

 remained a terror to 如何翻译是本句的难点。

My maternal grandmother, after having nine children who survived, one who died in infancy, and many miscarriages, as soon as she became a widow devoted herself to women higher education.

我外祖母有九个孩子活了下来,有一个孩子很小就死了,她还流产过多次。丈夫一死,她就致力于女子高等教育。

 句子的时间顺序如何在翻译中体现出来,这点对于初学翻译的同学非常重要。

Unit 5 Culture

She was one of the founders of Girton College, and worked hard at opening the medical profession to women.

她是戈登学院的创办人之一，曾竭力让医学专业对妇女开放。

注意 founders表示"创办人"；medical profession表示"医学专业"。

She used to relate how she met in Italy an elderly gentleman who was looking very sad.

她常对人说，她在意大利碰到过一位愁容满面的老先生。

注意 relate表示"说"；定语从句较短，采用前置译法。

She inquired the cause of his melancholy and he said that he had just parted from his two grandchildren.

她就问他为什么闷闷不乐，他说两个小孙孙刚刚离开他。

注意 代词在这里由上下文引导，所以可以直接翻译。

"Good gracious," she exclaimed, "I have seventy-two grandchildren, and if I were sad each time I parted from one of them, I should have a dismal existence!"

"我的天哪！"我外祖母就说，"我的孙子孙女有七十二个，要是每离开一个都要难过，我的生活可就太痛苦了。"

注意 Good gracious是一句古代时使用的英语；dismal existence表示"痛苦的生活"。

"Madre snaturale," he replied.

听了这话，老先生竟说："Madre snaturale。"[1]

第一个引号中是意大利语可以不翻译，表示中间语言。

But speaking as one of the seventy-two, I prefer her recipe.

但是我作为七十二人中的一员，倒是赞成她的办法的。

speaking as表示"涉及到"；recipe表示"办法"。

After the age of eighty she found she had some difficulty in getting to sleep, so she habitually spent the hours from midnight to three a.m. in reading popular science.

她过了八十以后，常睡不着觉，所以从午夜到凌晨三点总要读些科普读物。

popular science表示"科普读物"，不是"流行读物"。

I do not believe that she ever had time to notice that she was growing old.

我相信她从来没有工夫去注意自己是不是在日益衰老。

否定转移。

This, I think, is the proper recipe for remaining young.

我认为，要想永葆青春，这是最好的办法。

---

1 这句话是意大利语，意思是："这个做母亲的真怪呀！"

Unit 5　Culture

> **注意**　插入语表示的观点可以提到句首翻译。

　　If you have wide and keen interests and activities in which you can still be effective, you will have no reason to think about the merely statistical fact of the number of years you have already lived, still less of the probable brevity of your future.

　　你要是有广泛的爱好和强烈的兴趣，而且还有能力参加一些活动，你就没有理由去考虑自己已经活了多少岁这样的具体数字，更没有理由去考虑自己的余年大概是很有限的了。

> **注意**　定语从句较短，可以采用前置翻译；brevity翻译得比较具体。

　　As regards health, I have nothing useful to say since I have little experience of illness.

　　谈到健康问题，我就没有什么可说的了，因为我没怎么生过病。

 注意　as regards表示as for；experience可以弱化翻译。

　　I eat and drink whatever I like, and sleep when I cannot keep awake.

　　我想吃什么就吃什么，想喝什么就喝什么，眼睛睁不开了就睡觉。

 注意　本句翻译得十分口语化，比较简单易懂。

　　I never do anything whatever on the ground that it is good for health, though in actual fact the things I like doing are mostly wholesome.

我从来不为对身体有益而搞什么活动,然而,实际上,我喜欢做的事大多是有助于增进身体健康的。

> **注意** though这个单词的用法很有意思,注意如何翻译;wholesome表示"健康"。

Psychologically there are two dangers to be guarded against in old age.

从心理方面来说,到了老年,有两种危险倾向需要注意防止。

> **注意** 较长的形容词和副词可以单独翻译成句;被动语态不要用"被"翻译。

One of these is undue absorption in the past.

一是过分地怀念过去。

> **注意** absorption属于抽象名词,可以翻译为动词。

It does not do to live in memories, in regrets for the good old days, or in sadness about friends who are dead.

老想着过去,总觉得过去怎么好怎么好,或者总是为已故的朋友而忧伤,这是不妥的。

> **注意** 事实和评论的关系;句子翻译用了比较口语化的翻译方法。

One's thoughts must be directed to the future, and to things about which there is something to be done.

一个人应当考虑未来,考虑一些可以有所作为的事情。

被动语态的翻译方法,可以不用"被",翻译为"可以"。

This is not always easy; one's own past is a gradually increasing weight.

要做到这一点并非总是很容易的;自己过去的经历就是一个越来越沉重的包袱。

前面的this需要具体化翻译;标点符号仍然保留。

It is easy to think to oneself that one's emotions used to be more vivid than they are, and one's mind more keen.

人们往往会对自己说,我过去感情多么丰富,思想多么敏锐,现在不行了。

事实与评论的关系;断句也很重要。

If this is true it should be forgotten, and if it is forgotten it will probably not be true.

如果真是这样的话,那就不要去想它,而如果你不去想它,情形就很可能不是这样了。

被动语态的翻译;句中的代词需要具体化。

The other thing to be avoided is clinging to youth in the hope of sucking vigor from its vitality.

另一件需要避免的事就是老想和年轻人待在一起,希望从青年的活力中汲取力量。

 被动语态的译法；hope是典型的抽象名词，需要动词化。

When your children are grown up they want to live their own lives, and if you continue to be as interested in them as you were when they were young, you are likely to become a burden to them, unless they are unusually callous.

孩子们长大以后，就希望独立生活，如果你还像在他们年幼时那样关心他们，你就会成为他们的累赘，除非他们特别麻木不仁。

 when不要翻译为"当"；句型简单，形容词用得恰当，翻译也很独到。

I do not mean that one should be without interest in them, but one's interest should be contemplative and, if possible, philanthropic, but not unduly emotional.

我不是说一个人不应当关心孩子，而是说这种关心主要应该是多为他们着想，可能的话，给他们一些接济，而不应该过分地动感情。

 contemplative，philanthropic和emotional这三个形容词的翻译。

Animals become indifferent to their young as soon as their young can look after themselves, but human beings, owing to the length of infancy, find this difficult.

动物，一旦它们的后代能够自己照料自己，它们就不管了；但

Unit 5　Culture　　103

是人，由于抚养子女的时间长，是难以这样做的。

 注意 indifferent to不要翻译得过于生硬；difficult的翻译同样也是这个道理。

旧梦重温　Going Through Old Dreams

本文的作者是冰心，中国近现代最为著名的作家之一，其作品在中国广为流传。原名谢婉莹，笔名冰心，取"一片冰心在玉壶"为意。曾任中国民主促进会中央名誉主席，中国文联副主席，中国作家协会名誉主席、顾问，中国翻译工作者协会名誉理事等职，著名诗人、作家、翻译家、儿童文学家。本文选自于《光明日报》，记述的是她为王一地新书作序的事情，由庄绎传翻译。文中文学色彩较浓，翻译时意境成为较重要的问题。

王一地同志从1957年就当了中国少年儿童出版社的编辑，我们在多次"儿童文学"的聚会中早就认识了。

Comrade Wang Yidi became an editor of the China Children Press as early as 1957 and we came to know each other at the meetings held by "Children's Literature".

 注意 职称和姓名的位置关系；两个句子之间的连接很重要；"聚会"只能翻译为meeting，其他词不可以。

如今，能为他的这本散文集子作序，我觉得很荣幸。

I find it a great honour to be asked to write a preface to this collection of his essays.

注意 事实和评论的关系；被动语态的译法。

我必须承认，我的时间和精力似乎越来越少了。

I must admit that my time and energy seem to be running short.

 注意 中文分句之间需要联系；"越来越少"如何翻译。

一地同志送来的他的部分稿子，我不能仔细地欣赏，但我却充分感觉他的文章的魅力。

I was unable to read carefully and enjoy all the articles he had sent me, but I was fully aware of the charm of his writings.

 注意 中文句子的顺序；主语和宾语之间的关系。

如《海乡风情》写出了他对童年生活的眷恋。

In "Episodes in My Homeland near the Sea", he revealed his love for his childhood life.

 注意 英文没有书名号，用斜体或是双引号；主语的选择十分重要；代词的使用很重要。

《心上的河流》写出了他对于小河流水的深情，这使我忆起我所热爱的无边的大海。

In "A River at Heart", he expressed his deep feelings towards the flowing water of a creek, which reminded me of my own love for the boundless, vast sea.

注意 书名号和双引号的关系；"这"怎么翻译；"热爱的"和"无边的"之间是并列关系，在文学翻译中可以用逗号隔开。

他在国内旅游过的地方，除了井冈山以外，都是我没有到过的！

In China, he has been to many places which I have never visited, with the exception of the Jinggang Mountains.

 注意 "除了"怎么翻译，用词很讲究。

如丝绸之路上的阿克苏，青藏公路上的唐古拉、昆仑等，这又使我十分羡慕。

His trips to Aksu on the Silk Road, the Danggula and the Kunlun Mountains on the Qinghai-Tibet Highway and many other places all aroused my envy.

 注意 增加主语；句中专有名词要会翻译。

这几年来，我因行动不便，整天过着"井蛙"的无耻生活。

In recent years, unable to move about easily, I have been leading a dull life like that of "a frog at the bottom of a well".

注意 原因放在句子前部用形容词短语翻译；"井蛙"如何翻译。

读了这游记，绚丽生动得如经其境，给了我很大的快乐。

Reading his travel notes gave me great pleasure because they are so colorful and vivid that I felt I was actually there.

三个分句之间的关系；汉译英需要注意句与句之间的关系。

他到过的国外的地方，我在半个世纪以前就到过了，如伦敦、巴黎、罗马、佛罗伦萨等欧洲城市。

Overseas, he has been to places such as London, Paris, Rome and Florence in Europe, which I had visited half a century ago.

 Overseas放在句首和上文呼应；总分关系的翻译亦很重要。

虽然时代不同，我想历史古迹总该是依旧吧。

Times are different, but the historic sites, I presume, must have remained the same.

 转折词的翻译方法；插入语的翻译；时态的翻译。

如同旧梦重温一般，我回忆起1936年在伦敦的三个星期。

Just like going through old dreams, I remembered the three weeks I had spent in London in 1936.

 "旧梦重温"四字和题目相呼应。

在昼夜看不到日、月、星三光的浓雾之中，参观了大英博物馆、敏纳斯特教堂——访问了一些英国朋友。

During that time, when the sun, the moon and the stars were hidden behind the thick fog day and night, I visited the British Museum and the Westminster and called on my English friends.

Unit 5　Culture　107

注意　主动和被动的翻译；句子中的一些写作思路和当时中国的形势很相关。

使我喜欢的就是在这个国家到处都是绿茵茵的，比解放前的北京看上去舒服多了。

What I liked best was the refreshing green which could be seen all over the country. It was much more pleasant to the eye than Beijing before liberation.

注意　主语从句的翻译；"绿茵茵"该如何翻译；最后一个分句分开翻译是因为句与句之间没有关系。

提到巴黎，我永远忘不了我在那里逗留的100天。

Speaking of Paris, I could never forget the hundred days I had spent there.

注意　定语从句的翻译。

我住在第7区以意大利诗人马利亚·希利达命名的一条街的7层楼上（我在《关于女人》里写的《我的房东》说的就是我在巴黎那一段生活中的一部分）。

I lived on the sixth floor of a building in a street named after the Italian poet Maria Hilida in District 7 ("My Landlady" included in my book *About Women* was based on some of my experiences in Paris at the time).

注意　中西方语言在表达地点时的不同；后面括号内的语言仍然保留在原位，不改变位置。

因为住处离罗浮宫很近，我就整个上午"泡"在罗浮宫里。

As I was very close to the Louvre, I would loiter in the palace the whole morning.

 "泡"这个词该如何理解。

蒙娜丽莎的画像是悬挂在一条长案的上面，在两根绿色蜡烛的中间。

The portrait of Mona Lisa was hung above a narrow, long table with two green candles on either side.

 被动语态的使用；后面定语的翻译亦要注意。

我常常立在这长案旁边，吃我的简单早餐——一包巧克力糖！

I would often stand at the table having my simple breakfast——a bar of chocolate.

 "过去常常"用would；分句之间动词的处理很重要。

吃过早餐，就出来坐在宫门台阶上，欣赏宫门口那一座大花坛，花坛里栽的是红、黄、白、紫四色分明的盛开的郁金香！

After that, I would come out and sit on the steps at the entrance of the palace, enjoying the big flower beds near the gate filled with blooming tulips of distinctive red, yellow, white and purple.

 句子中的动词，译文中动词的处理很讲究，谁重要，谁不重要，要分清主次再进行翻译。

Literature (1)

Unit 6

Tess of the D'Urbervilles 德伯家的苔丝

本文作者是托马斯·哈代，英国诗人、小说家。他是横跨两个世纪的作家，早期和中期的创作以小说为主，继承和发扬了维多利亚时代的文学传统；晚年以其出色的诗歌开拓了英国20世纪的文学。本文摘选自哈代的主要作品——《德伯家的苔丝》，由张谷若翻译，[1]属于典型的文学作品，其中一些古老英语和方言英语的翻译较难，但很有特色，值得学习。

On an evening in the latter part of May a middle-aged man was walking homeward from Shaston to the village of Marlott, in the adjoining Vale of Blakemore or Blackmoor.

五月后半月里，有一天傍晚，一个中年男子，正打沙氏屯，朝着跟它相连的那个布蕾谷里面的马勒村往家里走去。

---

1 张谷若（1903—1994年），中国伟大的文学翻译家之一，在翻译领域取得了卓越的艺术成就，北京大学教授。他于20世纪30年代以成功地翻译了英国文学大师托马斯·哈代的代表作《德伯家的苔丝》和《还乡》一举成名。有七部、约400万言英国古典文学名著，除《苔丝》与《还乡》外，还有哈代的《无名的裘德》、狄更斯的《大卫·考坡菲》、亨利·菲尔丁的《弃儿汤姆·琼斯史》、莎士比亚的长诗《维纳斯与阿都尼》、肖伯纳的戏剧《伤心之家》以及唐诗英译等。

> **注意** 文学作品的断句；时间状语的顺序很重要；Shaston这个词翻译得很有中国特色。

The pair of legs that carried him were rickety, and there was a bias in his gait which inclined him somewhat to the left of a straight line.

支着他的那两条腿老是摇摇晃晃的，他走路的姿势里，又总有一种倾斜的趋势，使他或多或少地往一条直线的左边歪。

> **注意** 文学翻译需要理解意境，本句就是典型，要理解人喝酒喝醉之后是什么状态，并和中文相联系，再进行翻译。

He occasionally gave a smart nod, as if in confirmation of some opinion, though he was not thinking of anything in particular.

待一会儿他就轻快地把头一点，好像是对某一个意见表示赞成似的，其实他心里头可并没想什么特别的事儿。

> **注意** confirmation属于典型的抽象名词，需要翻译为动词；though的翻译需要仔细体会。

An empty egg-basket was slung upon his arm, the nap of his hat was ruffled, a patch being quite worn away at its brim where his thumb came in taking it off.

他胳膊上挎着一个空着的鸡蛋篮子，他头上那顶帽子的绒头都乱七八糟的，帽檐上摘帽子的时候大拇指接触的那个地方还磨掉了一大块。

> **注意** An empty egg-basket属于无灵主语，翻译为中文"他胳膊上"，属于有灵主语，要特别注意有灵主语句和无灵主语句的区别。

Unit 6　Literature (1)

Presently he was met by an elderly parson astride on a gray mare, who, as he rode, hummed a wandering tune.

他往前刚走了一会儿，就有一个上年纪的牧师，跨着一匹灰色的骒马，一路信口哼着一个小调儿，迎着面儿走来。

 本句的词汇和语法，原著的大部分英文现在已经不适用了。

"Good night t'ee", said the man with the basket.
"晚安，"挎篮子的人说。

 中古时期的英语。

"Good night, Sir John," said the parson.
"约翰爵士，晚安，"牧师说。

 本句无难点，直接翻译。

The pedestrian, after another pace or two, halted, and turned round.
那个步行的男子又走了一两步，站住了脚，转过身来。

 其中动作的连贯性和持续性。

Now, sir, begging your pardon; we met last market-day on this road about this time, and I zaid "Good night," and you made reply "Good night, Sir John," as now.

先生，对不起。上次赶集的日子，咱们差不多也是这样儿在这条路上碰见的，那回俺对你说"晚安"，你也跟刚才一样回答说"约翰爵士，晚安"。

> 注意 本句中"zaid"的翻译，这可以体现出主人公的特点。

"I did, "said the parson.

"不错，是，"牧师说。

> 注意 本句无难点，直接翻译。

And once before that——near a month ago.
I may have.

在那一次以前，大概有一个月了，也有过这么一回。
也许。

> 注意 本句无难点，直接翻译。

Then what might your meaning be in calling me "Sir John" these different times, when I be plain Jack Durbeyfield, the haggler?

俺分明是平平常常的杰克·德北，一个乡下小贩子，可你三番两次地老叫俺"约翰爵士"，到底是什么意思？

> 注意 其中方言的翻译，本句很有特色，让读者感觉出主人公的身份特征。

The parson rode a step or two nearer.

牧师拍马走近了一两步。

> 注意 nearer这个单词的语法知识，如何使用很重要。

Unit 6 Literature (1)   113

"It was only my whim, "he said; and, after a moment's hesitation: "It was on account of a discovery I made some little time ago, whilst I was hunting up pedigrees for the new county history."

"那不过是我一时的高兴就是了，"他说，跟着迟疑了一会儿："那是因为不久以前，我正考查各家的谱系预备编新郡志的时候，发现了一件事情，所以我才这么称呼你。"

 on account of 的翻译；后面句子翻译得很零乱，因为中文里善于按时间顺序翻译。

I am Parson Tringham, the antiquary, of Stagfoot Lane.
我是丝台夫路的崇干牧师兼博古家。

 同位语的翻译，可以用主谓译法。

Don't you really know, Durbeyfied, that you are the lineal representative of the ancient and knightly family of the d'Urberville, who derive their descent from Sir Pagan d'Urberville, that renowned knight who came from Normandy with William the Conqueror, as appears by Battle Abbey Roll?

德北，你真不知道你就是那古老的武士世家德伯氏的嫡派子孙吗？德伯氏的始祖是那位有名气的武士裴根·德伯爵士，据"纪功寺谱"上说，他是跟着胜利王维廉从诺曼底到英国来的。

 lineal表示"直系的"；that引导的是同位语。

Never heard it before, sir!
Well it's true.

从来没听说过,先生!
这是真事。

 这两句比较口语,直接翻译。

But you'll turn back and have a quart of beer wi' me on the strength o't, Pa' son Tringham?

可是,崇干牧师,既是这样,那你回来跟俺去喝它一夸特啤酒,好不好?

 wi'me表示 with me;o't表示of it;Pa'son表示Parson,以上这些口语都是没有知识的人的语言表达。

There's a very pretty brew in tap at The Pure Drop——though, to be sure, not so good as at Rolliver's.

清酒店有开了桶的好酒,可是比起露力芬店里的,自然还差点儿。

 The Pure Drop的翻译;Rolliver's表示商店名称。

No, thank you——not this evening, Durbeyfield. You've had enough already.

谢谢你,不喝了,今儿晚上不喝了,德北。我瞧你喝的已经不少了。

 这句话比较口语化,直接翻译。

An American Tragedy 美国悲剧

本文作者是西奥多·德莱塞，美国文学史上最杰出的现实主义小说家，一位以探索充满磨难的现实生活著称的美国自然主义作家。他的作品贴近广大人民的生活，诚实、大胆，充满了生活的激情。《嘉莉妹妹》真实再现了当时美国社会，而《美国悲剧》则是他成就最高的作品，让人们清晰地看到了美国社会的真实情况。本文摘选自《美国悲剧》第四章，由许汝祉翻译，[1]属于典型的文学翻译，特别是文中对于人物心理和性格的描写十分深刻，所以在翻译时注意用词。

Today, being driven by the necessity of doing something for himself, he entered the drug store which occupied the principal corner, facing 14th street at Baltimore, and finding a girl cashier in a small glass cage near the door, asked of her who was in charge of the soda fountain.

今天他因为急于要给自己想个办法，迫不得已，便走进了那家杂货店。这家店铺坐落在巴尔第摩街路口，正面是十四号街，地位正当要冲。他看见靠近门口的一座小玻璃柜房里有一个女出纳员，就去向她打听卖汽水的柜台归谁负责。

注意 分词位于句首，所以要先找主语；drug store是什么意思；定语从句该如何翻译。

---

[1] 许汝祉（1914年5月1日—2002年4月19日），江苏太仓人。1935年毕业于政治大学外文系。历任政治大学教授兼边疆学校副教授，安徽学院、南京师范大学教授，全国高等学校外国文学教育研究会副会长。长期从事外国文学的教学与研究工作，长于外国文艺理论研究与外国文学的翻译。曾开设《外国文学》、《西方现代派研究》、《西方文艺批评》、《美国文学史》等课程。主要译著有美国作家德莱赛的长篇小说《美国悲剧》、《马克·吐温自传》、《赫克尔贝里·芬历险记》等，主编《外国文学新观念》，编写《中国大百科全书》外国文学卷中的《德莱赛》词目，发表论文《异化文学与两种异化观》、《西方文学与人性论、人道主义》、《外国文学与文化》、《突破东西方文坛某种停滞的可能性》、《对美国后现代主义文学的评估》、《世界文学的教学与研究若干历史经验的探索》等。

Interested by his tentative and uncertain manner, as well as his deep and rather appealing eyes, and instinctively judging that he was looking for something to do, she observed: "Why, Mr. Secor, there, the manager of the store."

这个姑娘一看他那试探和踌躇的神情和他那双深沉的、相当讨人欢喜的眼睛，便对他发生了兴趣。她直觉地揣测到他是要找事做，便说："呕！塞科尔先生，在那儿，他是本店的经理。"

注意 分词Interested by位于句首，先找主语，再进行翻译；his tentative and uncertain manner, as well as his deep and rather appealing eyes，属于事实，Interested属于评论，注意事实和评论的关系；observed该如何翻译。

She nodded in the direction of a short, meticulously dressed man of about thirty-five, who was arranging an especial display of toilet novelties on the top of a glass case.

她朝一个三十五岁上下的矮个子男人那边点点头。那个人穿得很讲究，一点也不马虎。他正在布置一只玻璃柜上的一些新奇化妆品，要摆成一种特别的式样。

注意 meticulously dressed可以理解为长的副词词组，所以可以单独翻译；especial display的翻译方法也是一样。

Clyde approached him, and being still very dubious as to how one went about getting anything in life, and finding him engrossed in what he was doing, stood first on one foot and then on the other, until at last, sensing someone was hovering about for something, the man turned: "Well?" he queried.

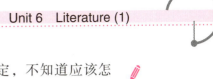

克莱德走到他身边，不过心里还在犹疑不定，不知道应该怎样才能找个出路，同时他又看出人家正在全神贯注地干他手头的事情，于是便站在一边，两只脚替换着歇一歇。到后来，那个经理觉得仿佛有人在他身边守着，想找他谈什么事，这才转过身来说："有事吗？"

> **注意** stood first on one foot and then on the other 该如何翻译，这点十分重要。

You don't happen to need a soda fountain helper, do you?
您这儿卖汽水的柜台上要不要添个助手？

> **注意** 附加疑问句的翻译，短的疑问句需要合成为一个长句来翻译。

Clyde cast at him a glance that said as plain as anything could, "If you have any such place, I wish you would please give it to me. I need it."
克莱德对他望了一眼，把自己的迫切心情表露得再清楚不过了。"要是有这样的位置，就请您让我来干吧。我想找这么个事情。"

> **注意** 定语从句的翻译 that said as plain as anything could。

"No, no, no ," replied this individual, who was blond and vigorous and by nature a little irritable and contentious.
"没有，没有，没有，"这个人回答说。他长得漂漂亮亮、精神饱满，生性有点暴躁，喜欢争吵。

> **注意** 句中四个形容词的翻译，这突出反映了这个男人的性格特征。

He was about to turn away, but seeing a flicker of disappointment and depression pass over Clyde's face, he turned and added, "Ever work in a place like this before?"

他正想走开，可是一看克莱德脸上掠过一阵失望和沮丧的神色，就转过身来说："从前在这种地方做过吗？"

> **注意** a flicker of disappointment and depression 属于无灵主语，翻译成中文"莱德脸上"为有灵主语，注意中英文有灵主语句和无灵主语句的翻译特点。

"No place as fine as this. No, sir." replied Clyde, rather fancifully moved by all that was about him.

"没有在这么讲究的地方做过。没有，先生，"克莱德回答说。这里的一切景象不免让他眼花缭乱，很感兴奋。

> **注意** 定语从句 that was about him 的翻译；如何反映主人公的心态需要仔细揣摩。

I'm working now down at Mr. Klinkle's store at 7th and Brooklyn, but it isn't anything like this one and I'd like to get something better if I could.

我眼下在七号街和布鲁克林街拐角，克林克尔先生店里帮忙。跟这儿比起来，那就算不上什么了，我要是能找到好一些的事，倒是很希望挪个地方。

Unit 6　Literature (1)　119

 本句无难点，直接翻译，但是要翻译出主人公的语言特点，突出他虚伪的特征。

"Uh," went on his interviewer, rather pleased by the innocent tribute to the superiority of his store.

"呕，"跟他谈话的这个人一听他这么天真地给他的铺子捧场，相当高兴。

 句子中by the innocent tribute to the superiority of his store是事实，rather pleased是评论，注意中英文事实与评论的关系；the superiority of的译法很有意思。

Well, that's reasonable enough. But there isn't anything here right now that I could offer you.

呕，这倒是人情之常。不过眼下我这儿没有什么事给你做。

 本句无难点，直接翻译，但是要注意口语化。

We don't make many changes. But if you'd like to be a bellboy, I can tell you where you might get a place.

我们不常换人。不过你要是愿意在饭店里做服务员，我倒可以告诉你上那儿去找个位置。

 bellboy表示"服务员"；注意口语化的翻译。

They're looking for an extra boy in the hotel inside there right now.

这里面的饭店眼下正要添个服务员。

本句无难点，直接翻译，但是要注意文学口语化的翻译。

The captain of the boys was telling me he was in need of one.
那儿的领班跟我说过，他需要找个伙计。

 captain在这里翻译为"领班"。

I should think that would be as good as helping about a soda fountain, any day.
我看这个差事总赶得上在卖汽水的柜台上当帮手吧。

 本句无难点，直接翻译，但是要注意文学口语化的翻译。

They seeing Clyde's face suddenly brighten, he added: "But you mustn't say that I sent you, because I don't know you."
他一看克莱德脸上突然露出喜色，又接着说："不过你千万别说是我介绍你去的，因为我并不认识你。"

 brighten的翻译；mustn't的使用要注意翻译说话人的语气。

Just ask for Mr. Squires inside there, under the stairs, and he can tell you all about it.
你只要上那里面去，到楼梯下面找史魁尔斯先生就行了，一切情形他会告诉你。

 本句无难点，直接翻译，但是要注意文学口语化的翻译。

祝福 The New Year's Sacrifice

本文作者鲁迅,伟大的文学家、思想家、革命家,是中国文化革命的主将。鲁迅先生一生写作计有600万字,其中著作约500万字,辑校和书信约100万字。作品包括杂文、短篇小说、评论、散文、翻译作品。对于"五四运动"以后的中国文学产生了深刻的影响。本文摘选自《鲁迅全集》第二卷,由杨宪益和戴乃迭共同翻译,[1]属于典型的文学作品,特别是在浙江官话的翻译上选词用句都恰到好处,属于经典之作,需要认真学习。

她不是鲁镇人。
She was not from Luzhen.

 注意 中文的地名该如何翻译。

有一年的冬初,四叔家里要换女工,做中人的卫老婆子带她进来了,头上扎着白头绳,乌裙,蓝夹袄,月白背心。
Early one winter, when my uncle's family wanted a new maid, Old Mrs. Wei the go-between brought her along. She had a white mourning band round her hair and was wearing a black skirt, blue jacket, and pale green bodice.

---

[1] 杨宪益(1915年1月12日—2009年11月23日)中国最著名的翻译家、外国文学研究专家、诗人。杨宪益曾与夫人戴乃迭合作翻译全本《红楼梦》、全本《儒林外史》、《楚辞》、《资治通鉴》等多部中国历史名著,在国内外皆获得好评,产生了广泛影响。其夫人戴乃迭,原名Gladys B. Tayler,婚后更名为Gladys Yang,1919年戴乃迭生于北京一个英国传教士家庭。戴乃迭七岁时返回英国,在教会中学接受教育。1937年戴乃迭考入牛津大学,最初学习法语语言文学,后转攻中国语言文学,是牛津大学首位中文学士。自20世纪40年代起定居中国,1999年11月18日戴乃迭于北京逝世。戴乃迭女士是中国文学出版社英籍老专家、在国际上享有崇高声誉的翻译家和中外文化交流活动家。

中文句子之间的逻辑关系;"中人"如何翻译;"乌"该如何翻译;"月白"的翻译也很有意思。

年纪大约二十六七,脸色青黄,但两颊却还是红的。

Her age was about twenty-six, and though her face was sallow her cheeks were red.

 英文是形合语言,句与句之间需要不同的形式来连接。

卫老婆子叫她祥林嫂,说是自己母家的邻舍,死了当家人,所以出来做工了。

Old Mrs. Wei introduced her as Xianglin's Wife, a neighbour of her mother's family, who wanted to go out to work now that her husband had died.

 "卫老婆子"如何翻译;"说是"表示同位语;"当家人"如何翻译;英文句与句之间需要连接。

四叔皱了皱眉,四婶已经知道了他的意思,是在讨厌她是一个寡妇。

My uncle frowned at this, and my aunt knew that he disapproved of taking on a widow.

 "皱眉"该如何翻译;英文句与句之间需要连接。

但看她模样还周正,手脚都壮大,又只是顺着眼,不开一句口,很像一个安分耐劳的人,便不管四叔的皱眉,将她留下了。

She looked just the person for them, though, with her big strong hands and feet; and, judging by her downcast eyes and silence, she was a good worker who would know her place. So my aunt ignored my uncle's frown and kept her.

> **注意** "周正"如何翻译；"安分耐劳"如何翻译；英文句子之间的层次非常重要，需要用不同的词汇进行连接。

试工期内，她整天的做，似乎闲着就无聊，又有力，简直抵得过一个男子，所以第三天就定局，每月工资五百文。

During her trial period she worked from morning till night as if she found resting irksome, and proved strong enough to do the work of a man; so on the third day she was taken on for five hundred cash a month.

> **注意** "无聊"如何翻译；"定局"如何翻译；句与句之间的连接及标点的使用都十分重要。

大家都叫她祥林嫂；没问她姓什么，但中人是卫家山人，既说是邻居，那大概也就姓卫了。

Everybody called her Xianglin's Wife and no one asked her own name, but since she had been introduced by someone from Wei Village as a neighbour, her surname was presumably also Wei.

> **注意** 中文善于用短句，英文善于用长句，句与句之间需要有连词。

她不很爱说话，别人问了才回答，答的也不多。
She said little, only answering briefly when asked a question.

句与句之间的连接词,用分词连接的手法很经典。

直到十几天之后,这才陆续的知道她家里还有严厉的婆婆;一个小叔子,十多岁,能打柴了。

Thus it took them a dozen days or so to find out bit by bit that she had a strict mother-in-law at home and a brother-in-law of ten or so, old enough to cut wood.

 "小叔子"该如何翻译;英文句子之间的连接很重要。

她是春天没了丈夫的;他本来也打柴为生,比她小十岁:大家所知道的就只是这一点。

Her husband, who had died that spring, had been a woodcutter too, and had been ten years younger than she was. This little was all they could learn.

 英文过去完成时态翻译很有特点;英文句子之间需要有连接。

日子很快的过去了,她的做工却毫没有懈,食物不论,力气是不惜的。

Time passed quickly. She went on working as hard as ever, not caring what she ate, never sparing herself.

 中文句子意群的区分,需要断句;"不惜"如何翻译。

人们都说鲁四老爷里雇着了女工,实在比勤快的男人还勤快。

It was generally agreed that the Lu family's maid actually got through more work than a hard-working man.

 英文句子之间的连接，特别是连词的使用。

到年底，扫尘，洗地，杀鸡，宰鹅，彻夜的煮福礼，全是一个人担当，竟没有添短工。

At the end of the year, she swept and mopped the floors, killed the chickens and geese, and sat up to boil the sacrificial meat, all single-hand, so that they did not need to hire extra help.

 并列动词如何翻译；"煮福礼"如何翻译；后面句子的连接很讲究。

然而她反满足，口角边渐渐的有了笑影，脸上也白胖了。

And she for her part was quite contented. Little by little the trace of a smile appeared at the corners of her mouth, while her face became whiter and plumper.

注意 中文句子意群的区分，需要断句；英文句子之间的连接很重要。

Unit 7 Literature (2)

East of Eden 伊甸之东

  本文作者约翰·斯坦贝克，20世纪美国最有影响力的作家之一。他熟悉社会底层的人们，其许多作品都以他们为主人公，表现了底层人的善良、质朴的品格，创造了"斯坦贝克式的英雄"形象。同时，他的小说艺术造诣很高，将写实风格与幻想风格有机地结合起来，对后来美国文学，尤其是西部文学的发展产生了重大的影响。其代表作品有小说《人鼠之间》、《愤怒的葡萄》、《月亮下去了》、《珍珠》、《伊甸之东》、《烦恼的冬天》等。本文摘选自《伊甸之东》第一章，由王永年翻译，[1]文中主要描述了作者故乡的美丽景色，用词十分优美，译者在翻译时选词独到，恰当地表达了原文的意思。

---

1 王永年（1927年3月17日—），笔名王仲年、雷怡、杨绮，1946年从上海圣约翰大学英国语文学系毕业，曾任中学俄语教师、外国文学编辑，1959年起担任中华人民共和国新华通讯社西班牙语译审，20世纪90年代中以正高级职称离休。他翻译新闻稿以精练、准确著名，到20世纪80年代中期稿件就已超过500万字，不论将中文翻译成西班牙文或西班牙文翻做中文都极为精到，广受欢迎。王永年精通英文、俄文、西班牙文、意大利文等多种外语，工作余暇翻译多种世界文学名著，以王仲年笔名翻译的系列欧·亨利小说，出版多种版本，畅销多年，历久不衰，备受英美文学研究者的好评。他又从意大利原文翻译意大利文学巨著《十日谈》和《约婚夫妇》，是中国从原文翻译《十日谈》的第一人。他翻译的英语文学作品还有诺贝尔文学奖美国得主约翰·史坦贝克（John Steinbeck）的《伊甸之东》（East of Eden）、辛克莱·刘易斯（Sinclair Lewis）的《巴比特》（Babbitt）。2005年，北京人民文学出版社推出他在2002年译完的《欧·亨利小说全集》共180万字，译介全部的欧·亨利作品给整个汉语世界。

Unit 7　Literature (2)

The Salinas Valley is in Northern California.
萨利纳斯河谷位于加利福尼亚州北部。

 Northern California的翻译，特别是north和northern的区别。

It is a long narrow swale between two ranges of mountains, and the Salinas River winds and twists up the center until it falls at last into Monterey Bay.
那是两条山脉之间的一片狭长的洼地，萨利纳斯河蜿蜒曲折从中间流过，最后注入蒙特雷海湾。

 winds and twists up表示"蜿蜒曲折"。

I remember my childhood names for grasses and secret flowers.
我记得儿时给各种小草和隐蔽的小花取的名字。

 names可以认为是抽象名词，所以可以增词。

I remember where a toad may live and what time the birds awaken in the summer——and what trees and seasons smelled like——how people looked and walked and smelled even.
我记得蛤蟆喜欢在什么地方栖身，鸟雀夏天早晨什么时候醒来——我还记得树木和不同季节特有的气息——记得人们的容貌、走路的姿态、甚至身上的气味。

 句子动词的翻译，可以转换词性为名词，looked and walked and smelled翻译为"人们的容貌、走路的姿态、甚至身上的气味"。

The memory of odors is very rich.

关于气味的记忆实在太多啦。

 本句无难点，直接翻译。

I remember that the Gabilan Mountains to the east of the valley were light gay mountains full of sun and loveliness and a kind of invitation, so that you wanted to climb into their warm foothills almost as you want to climb into the lap of a beloved mother.

我记得河谷东面的加毕仑山脉总是阳光璀璨、明媚可爱，仿佛向你殷勤邀请，你不禁想爬上暖洋洋的山麓小丘，正像爬到亲爱的母亲的怀里那样。

 full of sun and loveliness 翻译为"阳光璀璨、明媚可爱"；a kind of invitation 用明喻翻译。

They were beckoning mountains with a brown grass love.

棕色的草坡给你爱抚，向你召唤。

注意 本句需要意译，根据上下文的关系来翻译；特别注意 beckoning 的译法。

The Santa Lucias stood up against the sky to the west and kept the valley from the open sea, and they were dark and brooding——unfriendly and dangerous.

西面的圣卢西亚斯山脉高耸入云，黑压压地挡在河谷和大海之间，显得不友好而危险。

Unit 7　Literature (2)　　129

stood up against the sky翻译为"高耸入云"；keep...from可以用意译，不必翻译为"把……挡在……"。

I always found in myself a dread of west and a love of east.
我发现自己一直对西方怀有畏惧，而对东方怀有喜爱。

dread为抽象名词，翻译时要增词；而且动词要进行分配。

Where I ever got such an ideas I cannot say, unless it could be that the morning came over the peaks of the Gabilans and the night drifted back from the ridges of the Santa Lucias.
我说不出这种想法的根子在什么地方，也许是因为黎明从加比仑山顶升起，夜晚从圣卢西亚斯山脊压下来。

文学翻译中一些口语的翻译方法。

It may be that the birth and death of the day had some part it my feeling about the two ranges of mountains.
每一天的诞生和消亡也许让我对两条山脉产生了不同的感情。

本句无难点，直接翻译。

From both sides of the valley little steams slipped out of the hill canyons and fell into the bed of the Salinas River.
洼地两面的小峡谷都有涧水流出，汇入萨利纳斯河床。

little steams翻译为"涧水"；fell into翻译为"汇入"。

In the winter of wet years the streams ran full-freshet, and they swelled the river until sometimes it raged and boiled, bank full, and then it was a destroyer.

在多雨的年份，冬天水流充沛，引起河面暴涨，有时候汹涌翻腾，泛滥两岸，就成了祸害。

 full-freshet翻译为"充沛"；raged and boiled翻译为"汹涌翻腾"。

The river tore the edges of the farm lands and washed whole acres down; it toppled barns and houses into itself, to go floating and bobbing away.

河水冲坏了农田边缘，毁掉大片大片的土地，让牲口棚和房屋坍塌，卷入洪流，漂浮而去。

 whole acres翻译为"大片大片"；barns原意为"谷仓"，在这里翻译为"牲口棚"。

It trapped cows and pigs and sheep and drowned them in its muddy brown water and carried them to the sea.

牛、猪、羊走投无路，在黄褐色的泥水里眼睁睁地淹死，给带到海里。

 cows and pigs and sheep变为主语，句子更加通顺，且用拟人的手法；"眼睁睁地"也是拟人的手法。

Then when the late spring came, the river drew in from its edges and the sand banks appeared.

Unit 7　Literature (2)

春末时分，河面变窄，露出了沙岸。

 本句无难点，直接翻译。

And in the summer the river didn't run at all above ground.
到了夏天，地上河水完全断流。

 didn't run at all above ground直译是表示"没有在地面上流"，后来翻译为"断流"，更加准确。

Some pools would be left in the deep swirl places under a high bank.
只有原先岸高漩涡深的地方才留下几个水塘。

 本句被动语态使用了被动变主动的译法。

The tules and grasses grew back, and willows straightened up with the flood debris in their upper branches.
芦苇和茅草重新生长，柳树直起躯干，上部的枝桠还挂着洪水留下的枯枝败草。

 straightened up翻译为"直起躯干"，具有拟人特点；"洪水留下的"是根据上下文的增词。

The Salinas was only a part-time river.
萨利纳斯只是一条季节性河流。

 part-time river翻译为"季节性"河流。

The summer sun drove it under-ground.

夏天的太阳把它逼进了地底。

 drove翻译为"逼"。

It was not a fine river at all, but it was the only one we had and so we boasted about it——how dangerous it was in a wet winter and how dry it was in a dry summer.

它根本不是条了不起的河流，但是我们只有这么一条，因此便为它吹嘘——说它在多雨的冬天是多么危险，在干旱的夏天是何等枯竭。

 本句需要断句；标点需要保留；直接翻译。

You can boast about anything if it's all you have.

如果你别无他有，你可以为任何东西吹嘘。

 本句无难点，直接翻译。

Maybe the less you have, the more you are required to boast.

也许你有的东西越少，你就越要吹吹牛皮。

 "the+比较级，the+比较级"的翻译。

The Sound of Music 音乐之声

音乐之声（The Sound of Music）是一部改编自玛丽亚·冯·崔普的著作《崔普家庭演唱团》的戏剧作品，最初以音乐剧的形式于百老汇上演，之后改编成电影，获得第38届奥斯卡金像奖，其主题曲与电影同名。本文选自其中的一段，由庄绎传翻译，文章属于典型的文学翻译，以人物描写和环境描写居多，句型与用词十分讲究，译者在翻译时也体现了这一点。

Suddenly I heard quick footsteps behind me, and a full, resonant voice exclaimed:"I see you are looking at my flag."

我突然听见身后有急促的脚步声，接着就听见一个非常宏亮的声音说道："看来您是在看我的旗子哪！"

 句子中需要有敬语体翻译，"您"。

There he was——the Captain!
这个人——就是舰长！

 翻译时保留原有的标点符号。

The tall, well-dressed gentleman standing before me was certainly a far cry from the old sea wolf of my imagination.

站在我面前的是一位身材高大、衣着讲究的先生，与我先前想象的老海怪完全不同。

注意 分词位于名词后相当于定语从句；a far cry from翻译为"完全不同"。

His air of complete self-assurance and somewhat lordly bearing would have frightened me, had it not been for his warm and hearty handshake.

他和我握手的时候是那样热情，那样真挚，要不然他那十分自信的神气和略为高傲的派头真会让人害怕呢。

his warm and hearty handshake为无灵主语，翻译成中文为"他和我握手的时候是那样热情，那样真挚"为有灵主语，注意中英文有灵主语和无灵主语的翻译；had it not been for表示虚拟语气，翻译为"要不是"。

"I am so glad you have come, Fräulein…"
"你来了，我真高兴。小姐您叫……"

句子中的德语。

I filled in, "Maria."
我连忙说："玛丽亚。"

fill翻译为"说"。

He took me in from top to toe with a quick glance.
他以敏捷的眼光把我从头到脚打量了一番。

from head to toe表示"从头到脚"；take sb. in表示"打量某人"。

All of a sudden I became very conscious of my funny dress, and sure

Unit 7　Literature (2)　135

enough, there I was diving under my helmet again.

我突然强烈地感到自己这身衣服非常可笑。我真的又拉了拉帽子，想在帽子底下躲一躲。

 英译汉时先说主语；I was diving under my helmet again需要根据实际情况进行意译。

But the Captain's eyes rested on my shoes.
可是舰长的眼光却落到我的鞋上。

 rested on 表示"落在"。

We were still standing in the hall when he said: "I want you to meet the children first of all."

这时我们还在大厅里站着，他忽然说："我想让你先见见孩子们吧。"

 本句无难点，直接翻译。

Out of his pocket he took an odd-shaped, ornamented brass whistle, on which he piped a series of complicated trills.

他从口袋里掏出一个样子很怪但很精致的铜哨子，吹了一连串复杂的信号。

Out of his pocket在句首引起倒装；非限定性定语从句on which he piped a series of complicated trills采用后置译法。

I must have looked highly amazed, because he said, a little

apologetically: "You see it takes so long to call so many children by name, that I've given them each a different whistle."

我一定是显得很惊奇,因为他略带歉意地对我说:"你看,这么多孩子,要是一个个挨着叫名字,就得叫好半天,所以我就吹哨子,而且各有各的吹法。"

 apologetically这个副词的翻译;后面引号中的口语翻译值得关注。

Of course, I now expected to hear a loud banging of doors and a chorus of giggles and shouts, the scampering feet of youngsters jumping down the steps and sliding down the banister.

这时我想一定会听到"砰!砰!"的关门声,叽叽嘎嘎的说笑声,孩子们下楼时嘈杂的脚步声,他们一定是连跑加跳,有的还要顺着扶手滑下来。

 句中的象声词翻译得很讲究。

Instead, led by a sober-faced young girl in her early teens, an almost solemn little procession descended step by step in well-mannered silence——four girls and two boys, all dressed in sailor suits.

可是看见的却是一支小小的队伍,在一个十来岁的沉静的女孩子带领下,规规矩矩不声不响地磴磴走下来,简直可以说他们是非常严肃的。他们是四个女孩子,两个男孩子,都穿着水手服。

分词led by a sober-faced young girl in her early teens位于句首,先找主语再翻译;后面的同位语four girls and two boys, all选择了主谓的译法。

Unit 7　Literature (2)

For an instant we stared at each other in utter amazement.
我们以非常惊奇的眼光彼此看了片刻。

 utter表示"完全"。

I had never seen such perfect little ladies and gentlemen, and they had never seen such a helmet.
我从来没有见过这样出色的孩子，都像小女士、小先生一样，他们也从来没有见过我这样的帽子。

 perfect的翻译，其他无难点。

Here is our new teacher, Fräulein Maria.
这是我们新来的老师，玛丽亚小姐。

 本句无难点，有德语出现。

"Grüss Gott, Fräulein Maria," six voices echoed in unison.
"玛丽亚小姐，您好！"六个人齐声说道。

 本句中的德语翻译。

Six perfect bows followed.
（他们）接着又一本正经地鞠了六个躬。

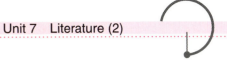 主语Six perfect bows为无灵主语，翻译为"他们"，成为有灵主语，注意有灵主语句和无灵主语句的翻译特点。

That wasn't real. That couldn't be true.

这不是真的。这不可能是真的。

 本句中that翻译为"这"。

I had to shove back that ridiculous hat again.

我不得不把那顶可笑的帽子又往后推一推。

 ridiculous的翻译。

This push, however, was the last.

不过这一推可就完了。

 转折词可以提到句首翻译。

Down came the ugly brown thing, rolled on the shiny parquet floor, and landed at the tiny feet of a very pretty, plump little girl of about five.

那棕色的丑东西一下子掉下来，在光亮的有图案地板上滚了一会儿，在一个大约五岁的胖乎乎的漂亮姑娘那双小脚旁停了下来。

 方位词Down位于句首引起倒装；中间一些形容词注意如何翻译。

A delighted giggle cut through the severe silence.

一阵咯咯的欢笑声打破了严肃而沉寂的气氛。

 severe silence后面增出的范畴词"气氛"。

The ice was broken. We all laughed.
谁也不拘束了，大家都笑了起来。

 The ice was broken 原意为"破冰"，后衍生为"不拘束"。

找点活　Looking for Work

本文作者新凤霞，评剧演员，是青衣、花旦，评剧新派创始人。原名杨淑敏，小名杨小凤，天津人，中共党员。6岁学京剧，12岁学评剧，14岁任主演。1949年后历任北京实验评剧团团长，解放军总政治部文工团评剧团副团长，中国评剧院演员，作家。全国第七届政协委员。本文选自于《新凤霞回忆录》，由杨宪益翻译，文中大量出现口语化和中国特色词汇，译文处理得十分得当妥帖，是难得一见的优秀译文。

在旧社会，我们评剧演员常常挣钱不够吃饭，艺人们大都是拉家带口，生活困难。

In the old society, pingju players seldom made enough to live on, and as most were saddled with big families their life was hard.

 句子之间的连接；句子中间有很多中国特色词汇，要注意使用。

演员们唱完戏还要各自找点儿活干，有人拉排子车，有人卖破烂，卖烟卷儿，当小工，拾烟头是普遍现象。

Apart from acting they had to find other work. Often they pulled handcarts, sold junk or cigarettes, hired themselves out as coolies, or collected cigarette stubs.

汉译英时要根据句子之间的意群进行断句;"普遍现象"属于评论性词,可以省略不译。

下雨或阴天回戏,不响锣就不给钱,是那时的规矩。

If a performance was cancelled because of bad weather, the rule in those days was: No show, no pay.

中文特色单词如何翻译,如"回戏"、"响锣"和"规矩"等;"不响锣就不给钱"翻译得很有英文特征。

腊月二十三封箱,把"祖师爷"请到前台去,后台冷冷清清,演员们就更苦了,要等到年初一开戏了,才能挣到钱。

On the twenty-third of the twelfth lunar month, when theatres closed and the patron saint of actors was invited to the front stage, leaving the backstage deserted, actors were even worse off, unable to earn any more until the reopening on New Year's Day.

中文特色的单词如何翻译,如"腊月二十三"、"祖师爷"和"年初一"等;句与句之间的连接亦很重要。

我家里生活苦,父亲做小买卖,妈妈是家庭妇女,弟弟妹妹多。

My family was hard up, with Father a peddler, Mother a housewife, and so many children to feed.

Unit 7　Literature (2)　　141

 句子中的同位语如何翻译；"父亲"与"母亲"在句中大写表示强调。

家里最大的是我，才十三岁，就唱戏养家了。
At thirteen, as the eldest child, I acted to help support the family.

 本句无难点，直接翻译。

真是一个钱撕成八瓣用，心里总想着怎样能够改善家里的困境。
Each single copper had to be eked out, and I kept racking my brains for ways to improve our difficult conditions.

 "撕成八瓣"如何翻译。

早晨去喊嗓子，我带着一个小篮拾煤核，为了回家取暖。
Each morning when I went out to practice singing in the open air, I took a little basket to scrounge for cinders for our stove.

 "喊嗓子"如何翻译；"回家取暖"翻译为for stove.

拾煤核也要放聪明点儿，常常换换地方，为的不受那些野男孩子的欺负，那些男孩子是成群结队的拾煤核。
Even when scrounging for cinders you had to have your wits about you and shift from place to place to avoid those mischievous boys who banded together to collect cinders too.

句子之间的连接；最后一个定语从句的翻译十分妥帖，将最后两个分句连接了起来。

我是一个人，怕被他们欺负，我用换地方的办法，躲着他们。

Being all on my own and afraid of being bullied by them, I shifted around to dodge them.

 寻找主语在汉译英时特别重要；句与句之间连接也很重要。

他们看见女孩拾煤核就捣乱，揪我的小辫，向我身上扔虫子，吓得我看见他们就躲。

Because when they found me scavenging they made trouble, pulling my plait or throwing insects at me, so that the sight of them frightened me away.

 句子之间的连接；动词之间的层次性；各种生词如何翻译。

腊月二十三灶王爷上天，后台封上戏箱，要等年初一开戏。

On the twenty-third of the twelfth month lunar the Kitchen God went up to the heaven, and the theatre shut down until New Year's Day.

 句中具有中文特色的单词翻译，如"灶王爷"、"封箱"和"开戏"等。

封箱回戏，等于演员们封嘴，大家可苦了。

When that happened, actors' pay stopped and they were hard put to it.

Unit 7　Literature (2)

 that指代上文"封箱";"可苦了"该如何翻译。

各自找生活路子,我们女孩儿就做点女孩子能做的活。
Each had to fend for himself, and we young actresses did whatever work we could pick up.

 "找生活路子"该如何翻译;"能做"翻译为pick up。

我同几个女孩子去东亚毛纺织厂当小工,分线头、扫地等干点杂活。
I went with some other girls to the East Asia Woolen Mill to do odd jobs like unraveling strands of wool or sweeping the floor.

 动词之间的关系;注意中英文之间总分关系的翻译,中文先分后总"当小工,分线头、扫地等干点杂活",英文先总后分to do odd jobs like unraveling strands of wool or sweeping the floor。

每天天不亮戴着星星去排队。
We had to queue up before dawn when there were still stars in the sky.

 "戴着星星"表示什么含义。

工厂没开大门就排上老长的队了。
A long queue formed before the mill's gate opened.

 主句与从句之间的关系。

工头拿着皮鞭从大门出来，像轰牲口一样轰人，一个挨一个地用粉笔在人们背上写上号码，

The foreman came out with a whip, as if herding cattle, and chalked a number on our backs, one by one.

"用粉笔写"直接翻译为动词chalked，十分生动；再注意句子中间的状语如何处理。

这个号码就是上工的证明。

That number showed that we were taken on.

"证明"如何翻译。

当这个小工真不容易。

But such small jobs were really hard to come by.

"当小工"如何翻译。

经常是排了一早晨队，大门才开；画了不多的号，工头就说："没号了！没号了！"

Often, when we'd queued up for hours before the gate opened, after chalking a few numbers the foreman would say, "That's all! No more hands needed!"

"经常"位于句首表示强调；"没号了！没号了！"翻译得很经典。

那种失望心情就别提多难受了！

Unit 7　Literature (2)　　145

At that we felt too disappointed for words!

 这里有灵主语和无灵主语的互换很有特色。

有一次是夏天，连阴天，连着回戏。我只好去排队找活干。

One summer a spell of bad weather closed down our theatre, and I went to queue up.

 前三个分句之间有联系，可以放在一起翻译；注意汉译英主语的寻找很重要。

还好，因为去得早，没等多久就画上号了。

I was lucky. Because I went early, before long I had a number chalked on my back.

 句子需要根据意群断句。

回家时忽然下了大雨，一路跑回家，我完全想不到自己被淋。

By the time we knocked off it was pouring with rain. As I ran home I didn't mind being soaked.

 句子之间的连接；汉译英句与句之间也需要断句。

只想着背上面的号，要是被雨淋掉，工就做不成了。

I was only worried that if the rain washed off the number on my back I wouldn't be able to go to work the next day.

 分句之间的连接，后两个分句之间用条件状语连接，很有特点。

我急着把衣服脱下来，大雨像瓢泼一样。

I frantically took off my gown, while it rained cats and dogs.

注意 "着急地"如何翻译；"瓢泼大雨"如何翻译。

我把衣服紧紧抱在怀里，飞快跑回家。回到家里打开一看就高兴了，号码一点也没有被淋湿；可我从头到脚淋成了落汤鸡了。

Clutching my gown to my heart I flew home, and there, unfolding it, I was overjoyed to find that the number wasn't washed out, though I was drenched from head to foot like a drowned rat.

注意 这句话中动词如何处理，并且多个句子合成一个句子翻译，难度较大；"落汤鸡"如何翻译。

Popular Science

Oil　　　　油

本文作者G. C. 索恩利，美国著名的科技小说家，以科普作品见长。本文选自于 *English Through Reading*，属于典型的非文学翻译，由庄绎传翻译。科技文献被动语态居多，本文主要学习被动语态的四种译法，可以结合《十二天突破英汉翻译（笔译篇）》同时学习。

There are three main groups of oils: animal, vegetable and mineral.
油可以分为三大类：动物油；植物油；矿物油。

> **注意**　形容词的分配原则。

Great quantities of animal oil come from whales, those enormous creatures of the sea which are the largest remaining animals in the world.
大量的动物油是从鲸鱼身上得来的。鲸鱼是海里的庞然大物，是世界上现有动物中最大的一种。

> **注意**　同位语的翻译采用主谓译法；定语从句采用后置译法。

To protect the whale from the cold of the Arctic seas, nature has provided it with a thick covering of fat called blubber.

大自然为了保护鲸鱼，让它不致在北冰洋受冻，便让它长了厚厚的一层脂肪，叫做鲸脂。

> **注意** 非谓语动词位于句首，先找主语再进行翻译；分词做定语的后置译法。

When the whale is killed, the blubber is stripped off and boiled down, either on board ship or on shore.

鲸鱼杀死之后，把鲸脂剥下来熬油，这项工作有的是在船上进行的，有的是在岸上进行的。

> **注意** 第一个分句被动语态的译法，运用了"有被不用被"的译法；再注意either...or...的翻译方法。

It produces a great quantity of oil which can be made into food for human consumption.

这样，就能生产出大量的油，供人们食用。

> **注意** 定语从句which can be made into food for human consumption的翻译；被动语态的翻译运用了"有被不用被"的译法。

A few other creatures yield oil, but none so much as the whale.

有些动物也出油，但都没有鲸鱼出得多。

> **注意** 比较级none so much as如何翻译。

The livers of the cod and the halibut, two kinds of fish, yield nourishing oil.

鳕鱼和比目鱼，这两种鱼的肝脏出的油营养丰富。

 同位语直接翻译；换主语的方法也值得注意。

Both cod liver oil and halibut liver oil are given to sick children and other invalids who need certain vitamins.

从这两种鱼得来的鱼肝油可以给缺少某种维生素的患儿或其他病人服用。

 被动语态的译法，在科技文献中，用"可以"来代替"被"字；定语从句who need certain vitamins的翻译。

These oils may be bought at any chemist's.

这两种鱼肝油在任何一家药房里都可以买到。

 these指上面的两种油；被动语态的翻译方法。

Vegetable oil has been known from antiquity.

植物油自古以来就为人们所熟悉。

 被动语态的"为所"译法。

No household can get on without it, for it is used in cooking.

任何家庭都离不开它，因为做饭的时候就要用它。

 被动语态的译法，运用了"有被不用被"的译法。

Perfumes may be made from the oils of certain flowers.

有花儿产生的油可以用来制造香水。

 被动语态的译法；在科技文献中，用"可以"来代替"被"字。

Soaps are made from vegetable and animal oils.

植物油和动物油还可以用来制作肥皂。

 被动语态的译法；在科技文献中，用"可以"来代替"被"字。

To the ordinary man, one kind of oil may be as important as another.

对一般人来说，这种油或那种油可能都是重要的。

 比较级as...as...的翻译方法。

But when the politician or the engineer refers to oil, he almost always means mineral oil, the oil that drives tanks, aero planes and warships, motor-cars and diesel locomotives, the oil that is used to lubricate all kinds of machinery.

但是，政客或工程师谈到油的时候，他所指的几乎总是矿物油。这种油可以用来开坦克，开飞机，开军舰，开汽车，开柴油机车，可以用来润滑各种机械。

 并列套用定语从句的译法；定语从句中存在被动语态时该如何翻译。

Unit 8 Popular Science

This is the oil that has changed the life of the common man.
就是这种油改变了普通人的生活。

> **注意** 定语从句 that has changed the life of the common man 的后置译法，the common man 如何翻译，在某年的考研完形填空中曾经出现过。

When it is refined into petrol it is used to drive the internal combustion engine.
这种油经过提炼变成汽油以后，可以用来开动内燃机。

> **注意** 被动语态的译法；在科技文献中，用"可以"来代替"被"字；internal combustion engine 如何翻译。

To it we owe the existence of the motor-car, which has replaced the private carriage drawn by the horse.
就是因为有了这种油，我们才能用上汽车，以代替马车。

> **注意** to it 位于句首倒装；the existence of 典型的抽象名词，注意如何翻译；后置定语从句翻译得很简单。

To it we owe the possibility of flying.
就是因为有了这种油，我们才有可能飞行。

> **注意** the possibility of 属于典型的抽象名词。

It has changed the methods of warfare on land and sea.
它还改变了陆战和海战的方法。

warfare的翻译方法。

This kind of oil comes out of the earth.

这种油来源于地下。

 本句无难点，直接翻译。

Because it burns well, it is used as fuel and in some ways it is superior to coal in this respect.

它因为易于燃烧，可以用作燃料，而且在这方面比煤还有若干优越之处。

 英译汉时先说主语；被动语态的翻译方法；在科技文献中，用"可以"来代替"被"字；is superior to的用法也要注意。

Many big ships now burn oil instead of coal.

现在许多大轮船就烧油而不烧煤。

 instead of的译法。

Because it burns brightly, it is used for illumination; countless homes are still illuminated with oil-burning lamps.

它因为燃烧时非常明亮，也可以用来照明，许多家庭现在仍靠油灯照明。

 被动语态的翻译；在科技文献中，用"可以"来代替"被"字；countless也可以翻译为"无数的"。

Because it is very slippery, it is used for lubrication.

它因为非常滑润，所以可以用作润滑剂。

注意 英译汉时先说主语；被动语态的翻译，在科技文献中，用"可以"来代替"被"字。

Two metal surfaces rubbing together cause friction and heat; but if they are separated by a thin film of oil, the friction and heat are reduced.

两个金属面相擦，就要产生摩擦和热；但如果在它们之间抹上薄薄的一层油，就可以减少摩擦，降低热度。

注意 分词在名词后该如何翻译；最后一个分句被动语态该如何翻译，在科技文献中，用"可以"来代替"被"字。

No machine would work for long if it were not properly lubricated.

任何机械如果不使用一定的润滑剂，就不能持续工作。

注意 英译汉时先说主语；虚拟语气该如何翻译。

The oil used for this purpose must be of the correct thickness; if it is too thin it will not give sufficient lubrication, and if it is too thick it will not reach all parts that must be lubricated.

润滑油的浓度必须适当，太稀则起不到应有的润滑作用，太稠则流不到所有需要润滑的零件。

注意 分词位于名词后相当于定语从句；后面两个条件状语从句的翻译亦很重要。

The Other Road 新路

本文作者雷切尔·卡森,美国海洋生物学家,但她是以她的小说《寂静的春天》(*Silent Spring*)引发了美国以至于全世界的环境保护事业。本文选自于这本书,由庄绎传翻译,属于典型的非文学翻译。文中生词较多,句式较难,在学习时一定要注意记忆生词和将句型分析到位。

We stand now where two roads diverge.
我们正处在两条道路分岔的地方。

 句中where引导的并不是定语从句,而是地点状语从句。

But unlike the roads in Robert Frost's familiar poem, they are not equally fair.
但是并不像我们所熟习的罗伯特·弗罗斯特诗中所说的,这两条路是同样的好。

 这句话中not equally fair该如何翻译,不译成否定,可以找到原诗,就知道后面为什么翻译成肯定了。

The road we have long been traveling is deceptively easy, a smooth super high-way on which we progress with great speed, but at its end lies disaster.
我们一直在走的这条路表面上很好走,是一条平坦的超级公路,我们可以高速前进,但是走到尽头却要遇到灾难。

 定语从句we have long been traveling的翻译;同位语a smooth super high-way的翻译。

Unit 8　Popular Science

The other fork of the road——the one "less traveled by"——offers our last, our only chance to reach a destination that assures the preservation of our earth.

另外一条路，是一条"走得不多"的路，它为我们提供最后的出路，也是唯一的出路，以便我们达到一定的目的，让我们这个地球确实得到保护。

 后置分词"less traveled by"的翻译；定语从句that assures the preservation of our earth的翻译；抽象名词preservation因为具有动词词根，可以直接翻译为动词"保护"。

The choice, after all, is ours to make.

走哪一条路，最终还是要由我们来选择。

 本句无难点，直接翻译。

If, having endured much, we have at last asserted our "right to know", and if, knowing, we have concluded that we are being asked to take senseless and frightening risks.

我们如果在忍受了很长时间之后，终于提出了"知情权"，我们如果知情以后，认为现在人们是在要求我们冒无谓的可怕风险。

 英译汉时先说主语；分词having endured much位于句首，先找出主语再进行翻译；被动语态we are being asked的翻译也很重要。

Then we should no longer accept the counsel of those who tell us we must fill our world with poisonous chemicals; we should look about and see what other course is open to us.

我们就不应该再听从那些人的建议，非得把我们这个世界弄得到处都是化学毒物，而应该往四下里看一看还有没有什么别的路。

 定语从句后置译法；poisonous chemicals该如何翻译。

A truly extraordinary variety of alternatives to the chemical control of insects is available.

（我们）除了用化学方法控制昆虫以外，还有其他各种非常奇妙的方法可以利用。

 A truly extraordinary variety of alternatives to the chemical control of insects为无灵主语，翻译为"我们"为有灵主语；alternatives的译法也很值得借鉴。

Some are already in use and have achieved brilliant success.
这些方法，有的已在使用，而且取得了显著的效果。

 再短的句子也要断句。

Others are in the stage of laboratory testing.
有的处于试验阶段。

 本句无难点，直接翻译。

Still others are little more than ideas in the minds of imaginative scientists, waiting for the opportunity to put them to the test.
有的则不过是富于想象力的科学家头脑里的一些想法，等到有

Unit 8　Popular Science　　157

机会的时候才能加以试验。

> **注意** 前两句和这句的关系，"一些，一些，另一些"翻译为 "some...others...still others..."。

All have this in common: they are biological solutions, based on understanding of the living organisms they seek to control, and of the whole fabric of life to which these organisms belong.

所有这些方法都有一个共同点：他们都是生物的解决办法，其基础是人们对所要控制的生物体的了解，以及对这些生物体整个生活状况的了解。

> **注意** 中间的分词based on understanding of the living organisms they seek to control变成名词翻译很有特点；定语从句to which these organisms belong的翻译也很有特点；各种名词的翻译需要注意。

Specialists representing various areas of the vast field of biology are contributing——entomologists, pathologists, geneticists, physiologists, bio-chemists, ecologists——all pouring their knowledge and their creative inspirations into the formation of a new science of biotic controls.

广博的生物学各个领域的专家，包括昆虫学家、病理学家、遗传学家、生理学家、生物化学家、生态学家，都在作出贡献，他们把自己的知识和创造性汇集起来，形成了一门新的科学——生物控制学。

> **注意** 各种专业名词的翻译；其中the formation of 属于典型的抽象名词，有动词根，直接翻译为动词"形成"。

"Any science may be likened to a river," says a Johns Hopkins biologist, Professor Carl P. Swanson.

霍普金斯大学生物学家卡尔·P.斯旺森教授说:"每一门科学都可以比做一条河。"

 说话人在中间或是末尾,都可以放在句首翻译。

It has its obscure and unpretentious beginning; its quiet stretches as well as its rapids; its periods of drought as well as of fullness.

其源头,隐隐约约,并不引人注目;其流势,时而平缓,时而湍急;其水情,有汛期,也有枯竭期。

 本句很具有文学翻译的特点,句型工整,特别注意形容词的翻译。

It gathers momentum with the work of many investigators and as it is fed by other streams of thought; it is deepened and broadened by the concepts and generalizations that are gradually evolved.

由于许多人从事研究工作,各种思想像支流一样注入其中,势头逐渐加强。新的概念和结论陆续产生,又让它得以加深和展宽。

 被动语态it is fed by other streams of thought的翻译;定语从句that are gradually evolved的翻译。

So it is with the science of biological control in its modern sense.

现代的生物控制学就是如此。

注意 so it is with的用法。

In America it had its obscure beginnings a century ago with the first attempts to introduce natural enemies of insects that were proving troublesome to farmers, an effort that sometimes moved slowly or not at all, but now and again gathered speed and momentum under the impetus of an outstanding success.

一百年前，这门科学在美国开始创立时也是隐隐约约的。当时有些昆虫给农民找麻烦，有人就试图以这些昆虫的天敌来对付。这项活动有时进展缓慢，甚至毫无进展，但有时一项突出的成就又推动它加快速度，让它突飞猛进。

注意 本句较长，可以先断句再翻译；the first attempts to中的attempt属于抽象名词，有动词词根直接翻译为动词"尝试"，后面定语从句that were proving troublesome to farmers的翻译也很有特点；本句较难，要仔细揣摩。

It had its period of drought when workers in applied entomology, dazzled by the spectacular new insecticides of the 1940's, turned their backs on all biological methods and set foot on "the treadmill of chemical control."

这门科学也有过枯竭期。在二十世纪四十年代，从事应用昆虫学的人看到新杀虫剂的显著效用，不禁为之眼花缭乱，便对生物方法冷眼相看，重新走上"化学控制的老路"。

注意 句首It需要指代清楚；句中一些重要专业名词的翻译需要注意；dazzled by the spectacular new insecticides of the 1940's相当于非限定性定语从句，可以放在原位翻译。

But the goal of an insect-free world continued to recede.

然而实现无昆虫的世界这一目标却越来越渺茫。

 本句无难点，直接翻译。

Now at last, as it has become apparent that the heedless and unrestrained use of chemicals is a greater menace to ourselves than to the targets, the river which is the science of biotic control flows again, fed by new streams of thought.

现在已经很明显，盲目地大量使用化学杀虫剂，对我们自己的威胁比对要控制的对象的威胁还要大，于是，生物控制学这一条河又流动起来，而且有新的思想支流注入其中。

the heedless and unrestrained use of chemicals 中的 use 是抽象名词，有动词词根需要翻译为动词；最后一句的过去分词按照定语从句翻译。

Some of the most fascinating of the new methods are those that seek to turn the strength of a species against itself——to use the drive of an insect's life forces to destroy it.

在这些新方法中，有一些最为令人神往，就是设法利用一种昆虫本身的力量来对付这种昆虫，即利用昆虫的生命力作为动力来消灭之。

本句需要断句；定语从句 that seek to turn the strength of a species against itself 的翻译很重要。

The most spectacular of these approaches is the "male sterilization" technique developed by the chief of the United States Department of Agriculture's Entomology Research Branch, Dr. Edward Knipling, and his associates.

这些方法之中，最引人注目的是"雄性不育"术，这种技术是由美国农业部昆虫研究所主任爱德华·尼普林博士和他的同事们发明的。

> **注意** 本句需要断句；过去分词developed by the chief of the United States Department of Agriculture's Entomology Research Branch, Dr. Edward Knipling, and his associates翻译为定语从句；同位语the chief of the United States Department of Agriculture's Entomology Research Branch, Dr. Edward Knipling直接翻译。

海洋可持续发展战略
Sustainable Marine Development Strategy

本文作者不详，摘自于《中国海洋事业的发展》第一部分，来源于《北京周报》，译者不详，属于典型的非文学翻译。文中海洋类词汇较多，句式比较复杂，注意译者在处理句式时的方法和技巧。

中国有12亿多人口，陆地自然资源人均占有量低于世界平均水平。
China has a population of more than 1.2 billion, and its land natural resources per capita are lower than the world's average.

> **注意** "拥有人口"如何翻译；"水平"为范畴词，可省略；句与句之间需要连接。

根据中国有关方面的统计：中国有960万平方公里的陆地国土，居世界第三位。

Official statistics show that China has a land area of 9.6 million sq km, making it the third-biggest country in the world.

 "根据"可以不翻译为according to；"方面"为范畴词，可省略；动词之间的层次性很重要。

但人均占有陆地面积仅有0.008平方公里，远低于世界人均0.3平方公里的水平。

However, the land area per capita is only 0.008 sq km, much lower than the world's average of 0.3 sq km per capita.

 "人均"如何翻译；句与句之间如何连接。

全国近年来年平均淡水资源总量为28 000亿立方米，居世界第六位，但人均占有量仅为世界平均水平的四分之一。

In recent years China's average annual amount of freshwater resources has been 2,800 billion cu m, ranking sixth in the world, but the amount of freshwater resources per capita is only one-fourth the world average.

 数量单位的翻译；句与句之间的连接，可以用分词，也可以用连词。

中国陆地矿产资源总量丰富，但人均占有量不到世界人均量的一半。

China is rich in land mineral resources, but the amount per capita is

Unit 8　Popular Science　　163

less than half the figure per capita worldwide.

 "在……丰富"如何翻译;"世界"翻译得很巧妙。

中国作为一个发展中的沿海大国,国民经济要持续发展,必须把海洋的开发和保护作为一项长期的战略任务。

As a major developing country with a long coastline, China, therefore, must take exploitation and protection of the ocean as a long-term strategic task before it can achieve the sustainable development of its national economy.

谓语动词的层次性,判断每个中文句子中动词之间的关系是汉译英的核心问题;"长期战略任务"如何翻译;"持续发展"如何翻译;句与句之间的关系如何处理。

中国拥有大陆岸线18 000多公里。

China boasts a mainland coastline of more than 18,000 km.

 "拥有"如何翻译。

以及面积在500平方米以上的海岛5000多个,岛屿岸线14 000多公里。

There are more than 5,000 islands in China's territorial waters, each with an area of more than 500 sq m, and the islands' coastlines total more than 14,000 km.

注意 这句和上句相连,"以及"如何处理,不能都翻译为with;"达到"可以直接用动词total。

按照《联合国海洋法公约》的规定,中国还对广阔的大陆架和专属经济区行使主权权利和管辖权。

China also exercises sovereignty and jurisdiction over the vast continental shelves and exclusive economic zones (EEZs), as defined by the UN Convention on the Law of the sea.

"行使主权和管辖权"如何翻译;"专属经济区"如何翻译;"按照"如何翻译。

中国的海域处在中、低纬度地带,自然环境和资源条件比较优越。

Located in medium and low latitudes, China's sea areas have comparatively advantageous natural environmental and resource conditions.

处理句与句之间动词的关系;分词位于句首处理了前后两个分句之间的关系。

中国海域海洋生物物种繁多,已鉴定的达20 278种。

Some 20, 278 species of sea creatures have been verified there.

本句使用了被动语态的译法,符合科技文献的特点。

中国海域已经开发的渔场面积达81.8万平方海里。

The fishing grounds that have been developed in China's sea areas cover 818,000 square nautical miles.

注意
定语从句"已经开发的"的翻译;"平方海里"如何翻译。

Unit 8　Popular Science　　165

　　中国有浅海、滩涂总面积约1 333万公顷，按现在的科学水平，可进行人工养殖的水面有260万公顷，已经开发利用的有93.8万公顷。

　　The shallow seas and tidelands have a total area of 13.33 million ha, of which 2.6 million ha of water surface are suitable for the raising of aquatic products in terms of the current scientific level. So far, 938,000 ha are being utilized for this purpose.

> **注意** 插入语可以放在句首或是句末翻译；句与句之间使用了定语从句的方法来连接；最后一个分句处理为第二句。

　　中国海域有30多个沉积盆地，面积近70万平方公里。

　　Scattered in these offshore waters are more than 30 sedimentation basins, with a total area of nearly 700, 000 sq km.

> **注意** "沉积盆地"如何翻；句与句之间的连接很重要。

　　石油资源量约250亿吨，天然气资源量约8.4万亿立方米。

　　It is estimated that there are about 25 billion tons of oil resources and 8.4 trillion cu m of natural gas in these basins.

> **注意** 句前增词"It is estimated that"；句与句之间用with连接很恰当。

　　中国沿海共有160多处海湾和几百公里深水岸线，许多岸段适合建设港口，发展海洋运输业。

　　More than 160 bays are spread along China's coasts, plus the deep-water stretches of coast with a total length of several hundred kilometers. Many spots along the coastline are suitable for constructing harbors and developing marine transportation.

> **注意** "中国沿海共有160多处海湾和几百公里深水岸线"可以翻译为被动语态；前两句之间使用了plus连接；最后一个分句则是分开翻译。

沿海地区共有1 500多处旅游娱乐景观资源，适合发展海洋旅游业。

There are more than 1,500 tourist, scenic and recreational spots favorable for developing marine tourism.

> **注意** there be句型的使用；后一个分句用形容词短语连接。

中国海域还有丰富的海水资源和海洋可再生能源。

In addition, China's offshore areas abound in seawater resources and regenerable marine energy resources.

> **注意** "丰富"如何处理；专业名词"海水资源"和"海洋可再生能源"该如何翻译。

Law

Environmental Law 环境保护法

本文作者不详，选自于陈忠诚选编的《法律英语五十篇》，[1]属于典型的非文学翻译。法律翻译是非文学翻译的重要分支，要求内容紧密，语言精确，特别强调忠实于原文，不改变句子结构，以十分准确和简练的语言来传达原意。

As recently as the early 1960s, the phrase "environmental law" would probably have produced little more than a puzzled look, even from many lawyers.

早在六十年代初，甚至连许多律师接触到"环保法"这个词儿，大半也只会感到纳闷而已。

---

1 陈忠诚，号中绳（1922年—）。上海圣约翰大学经济系肄业，东吴大学中国比较法学院法学士（1947年）、比较法硕士（1949年）、大学本科毕业前在美国独资企业德士古石油公司中国公司法律部任兼职法律翻译，毕业后任专职法律顾问。1951年起，任最高人民法院华东分院编纂、华东司法改革办公室工作人员。华东政法学院成立后，在该院任教，为原经济法系教授，兼法律学术交流的俄语（50年代）、英语（70年代）和日语（90年代中）口译。1992年退休后任上海大学法学院终身教授。2000年6月出版了《法苑译谭》一书，该书内容既涉及法律（学）文字之英译汉，亦涉及其汉译英，并予后者以重视——因为它是外向型的，直接影响我国法律之国际形象，而且是较之内向型法律翻译更为薄弱的环节，是法律（学）翻译的新天地。

> the phrase "environmental law" 为无灵主语，翻译为"甚至连许多律师"为有灵主语，注意两者之间的互换翻译。

Such issues as clean air, pure water and freedom from noise pollution were not important public concern.

当时，诸如空气清新、水质洁净、无噪声污染之类的问题，都不是公众怎么了不起的关切所在。

> 本句的断句很重要；public concern表示"公众关切"。

There were, of course, numerous state and some federal laws intended to protect America's rivers and streams from excessive industrial pollution and to guard wildlife from the depredations of man.

当然，已经有了许多州法和一些联邦法，其立法意图是保护美国的江河，使之免受过分的工业污染并保护野生生物不受人类的掠夺。

> 插入语of course表示观点，可以提到句首翻译；分词intended to protect America's rivers and streams from excessive industrial pollution位于名词后相当于定语从句；from 有"趋利避害"的意思。

But these regulations were generally ignored.

可是对这些规定，人们一般都置之不理。

> 被动语态的翻译，用被动语态变成主动语态的译法。

With enforcement power dispersed among many federal, state and local agencies, most of which were seriously undermanned, and with noncompliance penalties so slight as to have little more than harassment value, there were few incentives to obey the laws.

由于执法的权力分散在许许多多的联邦、州和地方等三级机关（而这些机关大多人手严重不足），也由于因违法而科处的罚款微不足道（从而只有恼人心烦的意义），人们就缺乏服从法律的劲头了。

> **注意** 非限定性定语从句most of which were seriously undermanned放在括号里翻译，在法律英语中常见；最后一句需要找到主语再进行翻译。

Indeed, many environmental statutes were so little publicized and so vaguely worded that their existence was hardly known and their meaning was scarcely understood.

说真的，许多环境法的宣传工作之薄弱与措词之含糊，让人简直不知道有环境法，而环境法的意义也就无人了解了。

> **注意** 陈忠诚先生用了"之"字结构，引起定语的后置现象；that后的被动语态翻译需要注意。

Then, in 1962, came a book called *Silent Spring* by Rachel Carson.

不久以后，在1962年雷切尔·卡森所著、名为《沉默的春天》一书问世了。

> **注意** 中英文书名的书写方法；本句英文是完全倒装的结构，在翻译时需要注意。

A powerful indictment of America's disregard of ecology, *Silent*

Spring was aimed chiefly at the wholesale use of chemical pesticides, especially DDT.

《沉默的春天》有力地控诉了美国之忽视生态，它主要是针对大规模使用农药——特别是滴滴涕。

> **注意** indictment属于典型的抽象名词，有动词词根时，翻译时需要改成动词；第一个逗号后的被动语态的翻译需要注意；use属于典型的抽象名词，有动词词根时，翻译时需要改成动词。

In 1965 a court action took place that ranks in environmental importance with the publication of *Silent Spring*.

1965年又发生了一件诉讼，其对环境之重要意义，不亚于《沉默的春天》的出版。

> **注意** 定语从句that ranks in environmental importance with the publication of Silent Spring的翻译。

That was the reversal by a court of appeals of a Federal Power Commission decision to grant a license for a Consolidated Edison power plant at Storm King Mountain on the Hudson River in New York.

某上诉法院驳回了联邦电力委员会关于向纽约哈得逊河畔施多姆金山爱迪生联合发电厂颁发许可的决定。

> **注意** 本句开头的that是承接上一句的；句中的定语和状语较多，注意排序。

The court ordered new proceedings that were to "include as a basic concern the preservation of natural beauty and of national historic shrines".

该法院命重新处理该案并"以保护自然美和历史名胜为基本注意事项"。

> **注意** 本句that所引导的定语从句的翻译；basic concern表示"基本注意事项"；preservation为典型的抽象名词，有动词词根，直接翻译为动词"保护"。

UNIVERSAL COPYRIGHT CONVENTION (Excerpt)
《世界版权公约》（节选）

本文节选自《世界版权公约》，译者不详，属于典型的法律条文翻译，句式较长，且意思晦涩难懂，在翻译时要注意语言简练准确。

The Contracting States,

Moved by the desire to ensure in all countries copyright protection of literary, scientific and artistic works,

各成员国：

出于保证其各国对文学、科学及艺术作品的版权予以保护的愿望，

> **注意** 翻译法律文件时，需要注意前面过去分词的作用，基本不改变词性，直接翻译。

Convinced that a system of copyright protection appropriate to all nations of the world and expressed in a universal convention, additional to, and without impairing international systems already in force, will ensure respect for the rights of the individual and encourage the development of literature, the sciences and the arts,

确信适用于世界各国并以某种世界公约确定下来的用以补充而不是损害现行国际制度的版权保护制度，将保证对个人权利的尊重及鼓励文学、科学与艺术的发展，

> **注意** 形容词短语appropriate to all nations of the world and expressed in a universal convention位于名词a system of copyright protection之后相当于定语从句，但是不能根据长短改变语序，需要全部提前翻译，这是法律英语的特点。

Persuaded that such a universal copyright system will facilitate a wider dissemination of works of the human mind and increase international understanding,

相信这种世界版权保护制度将促进人类精神产品更加广泛的传播，将增进国际了解；

> **注意** 本句直接翻译，甚至连逗号都要少给，不要盲目加逗号，否则会产生歧义。

Have resolved to revise the Universal Copyright Convention as signed at Geneva on 6 September 1952 (hereinafter called "the 1952 Convention"), and consequently,

故决定修订1952年9月6日于日内瓦签订的《世界版权公约》（下称"1952年公约"），

> **注意** hereinafter called是典型的法律英语。

Have agreed as follows:

达成如下协议：

法律英语的固定表达法。

ARTICLE I
第一条

Each Contracting State undertakes to provide for the adequate and effective protection of the rights of authors and other copyright proprietors in literary, scientific and artistic works, including writings, musical, dramatic and cinematographic works, and paintings, engravings and sculpture.

各成员国承担对文学、科学及艺术作品（包括文字的、音乐的、戏剧的、电影的作品，以及绘画、雕刻与雕塑）的作者及其他版权所有者的权利提供充分、有效的保护。

专业名词的翻译；undertakes to provide for属于谓语动词的过渡。

ARTICLE II
第二条

1. Published works of nationals of any Contracting State and works first published in that State shall enjoy in each other Contracting State the same protection as that other State accords to works of its nationals first published in its own territory, as well as the protection specially granted by this Convention.

（一）任何成员国国民的已出版的作品，任何于该成员国首次出版的作品，在其他成员国中均享有后者给予其本国国民首次于本国地域内出版之作品同等的保护，并享有本公约所专门授予的保护。

the same...as是本句翻译最关键的词组，词组前后成分不改变位置。

2. Unpublished works of nationals of each Contracting State shall enjoy in each other Contracting State the same protection as that other State accords to unpublished works of its own nationals, as well as the Protection specially granted by this Convention.

（二）任何成员国国民未出版的作品，在其他各成员国中均享受有后者给予其国民之未出版的作品同等的保护，并享有本公约所专门授予的保护。

本句和上一句一样，中间表示"相同的"这个词组是翻译的根本。

3. For the purpose of this Convention any Contracting State may, by domestic legislation, assimilate to its own nationals any person domiciled in that State.

（三）为实施本公约，任何成员国均可按照国内立法，将经常居住于该国的任何人按本国国民对待。

domicile是个很有用处的词汇。

《中华人民共和国中外合资经营企业法》
LAW OF THE PEOPLE'S REPUBLIC OF CHINA ON CHINESE –FOREIGN EQUITY JOINT VENTURES

本文选自于《中华人民共和国中外合资经营企业法》，译者不详，属于典型的法律条文翻译，生词较多，句式较难，可以认为是本书中最难的一篇课文，但是翻译方法体现较多，在学习时要多注意句式的变化。

（1979年7月1日第五届全国人民代表大会第二次会议通过，根据1990年4月4日第七届全国人民代表大会第三次会议《关于修改〈中华人民共和国中外合资经营企业法〉的决定》修正）

(Adopted at the Second Session of the Fifth National People's Congress on July 1, 1979, and revised in accordance with the Decision of the National People's Congress Regarding the Revision of the Law of the People's Republic of China on Chinese-Foreign Equity Joint Ventures adopted at the Third Session of the Seventh National People's Congress on April 4,1990)

> **注意** 其中的专业名词的翻译，如"全国人大"和"中华人民共和国中外合资经营企业"等；而且时间、地点状语的排序亦很重要，仔细学习。

第一条　中华人民共和国为了扩大国际经济合作和技术交流，允许外国公司、企业和其他经济组织或个人（以下简称外国合营者），按照平等互利的原则，经中国政府批准，在中华人民共和国境内，同中国的公司、企业或其他经济组织（以下简称中国合营者）共同举办合营企业。

Article 1　With a view to expanding international economic cooperation and technological exchange, the People's Republic of China permits foreign companies, enterprises, other economic organizations or individuals (hereinafter referred to as "foreign joint venturers") to establish equity joint ventures together with Chinese companies, enterprises or other economic organizations (hereinafter referred to as "Chinese joint venturers") within the territory of the People's Republic of China on the principle of equality and mutual benefit and subject to approval by the Chinese Government.

> **注意**　中文先说主语，再说辅助语，英文刚好相反；其中专业名词的翻译很重要，如"国际经济合作"、"技术交流"、"外国公司"、"企业"和"其他经济组织或个人"等；状语的排序也很重要。

第二条　中国政府依法保护外国合营者按照经中国政府批准的协议、合同、章程在合营企业的投资、应分得的利润和其他合法权益。

Article 2　The Chinese Government protects, according to the law, the investment of foreign joint venturers, the profits due them and their other lawful rights and interests in an equity joint venture, pursuant to the agreement, contract and articles of association approved by the Chinese Government.

> **注意**　中文先说主语，再说辅助语，英文刚好相反；其中专业名词，如"协议"、"合同"和"章程"等词的翻译很重要。

合营企业的一切活动应遵守中华人民共和国法律，法令和有关条例的规定。

All activities of an equity joint venture shall comply with the provisions of the laws, decrees and pertinent regulations of the People's Republic of China.

 本句可以换主语，也可以不换；"的规定"的"的"究竟是修饰前面一部分还是全部，需要注意。

国家对合营企业不实行国有化和征收；在特殊情况下，根据社会公共利益的需要，对合营企业可以依照法律程序实行征收，并给予相应的补偿。

The State shall not nationalize or requisition any equity joint venture. Under special circumstances, when pubic interest requires, equity joint ventures may be requisitioned by following legal procedures and appropriate compensation shall be made.

中文里分号相当于英文里句号；最后一句中文"并给予相应的补偿"可以翻译为被动语态，从英文被动语态到中文不难，但是从中文看出被动语态却不容易。

第三条　合营各方签订的合营协议、合同、章程，应报国家对外经济贸易主管部门（以下称审查批准机关）审查批准。

Article 3 The equity joint venture agreement, contract and articles of association signed by the parties to the venture shall be submitted to the State's competent department in charge of foreign economic relations and trade (hereinafter referred to as the examination and approval authorities) for examination and approval.

注意 "应报"应该理解为被动语态；专业名词，如"合营协议"、"合同"和"章程"等词的翻译亦很重要。

审查批准机关应在三个月内决定批准或不批准。
The examination and approval authorities shall decide to approve or disapprove the venture within three months.

注意 shall的使用是典型的法律英语。

合营企业经批准后，向国家工商行政管理主管部门登记，领取营业执照，开始营业。
When approved, the equity joint venture shall register with the State's competent department in charge of industry and commerce administration, acquire a business license and start operations.

注意 中文先说主语，再说辅助语，英文刚好相反；汉译英时句与句之间的连接更加重要。

第四条 合营企业的形式为有限责任公司。
Article 4 An equity joint venture shall take the form of a limited liability company.

注意 换主语，汉译英时主语过长，且出现偏正短语时，取偏做主语。

在合营企业的注册资本中，外国合营者的投资比例一般不低于百分之二十五。

The proportion of the foreign joint venturer's investment in an equity joint venture shall be, in general, not less than 25 percent of its registered capital.

 专业名词"注册资本"和"投资比例"的翻译。

合营各方按注册资本比例分享利润和分担风险及亏损。

The parties to the venture shall share the profits, risks and losses in proportion to their contributions to the registered capital.

 "分担"和"分享"属于同一动词，可以抽象出来翻译为一个动词。

合营者的注册资本如果转让必须经合营各方同意。

If any of the joint venturers wishes to assign its registered capital, it must obtain the consent of the other parties to the venture.

 本句需要找到中文的主语，在汉译英时找到主语十分关键；而且要分清动词"转让"和"同意"之间的关系。

第五条　合营企业各方可以现金、实物、工业产权等进行投资。

Article 5 The parties to an equity joint venture may make their investment in cash, in kind or in industrial property rights, etc.

 make their investment属于典型的过渡形式；"实物"翻译为in kind。

外国合营者作为投资的技术和设备，必须确实是适合我国需要的先进技术和设备。

The technology and equipment contributed by a foreign joint venturer as its investment must be really advanced technology and equipment that suit China's needs.

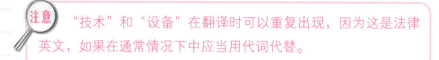
"技术"和"设备"在翻译时可以重复出现，因为这是法律英文，如果在通常情况下中应当用代词代替。

如果有意以落后的技术和设备进行欺骗，造成损失的，应赔偿损失。

In case of losses caused by a foreign joint venturer in its practicing deception through the intentional provision of outdated technology and equipment, it shall compensate for the losses.

第一个分句应该怎样和后一个分句连接。

中国合营者的投资可包括为合营企业经营期间提供的场地使用权。

A Chinese joint venturer's investment may include the right to the use of a site provided for the equity joint venture during the period of its operation.

定语"提供的"、"场地"、"使用的"该如何翻译。

如果场地使用权未作为中国合营者投资的一部分，合营企业应向中国政府缴纳使用费。

If the right to the use of the site is not taken as a part of the Chinese joint venturer's investment, the equity joint venture shall pay the Chinese

Government for its use.

> **注意** 条件句"如果场地使用权未作为中国合营者投资的一部分"的使用和shall的使用。

上述各项投资应在合营企业的合同和章程中加以规定，其价格（场地除外）由合营各方评议商定。

The above-mentioned investments shall be specified in the contract and articles of association of the equity joint venture and their value (excluding that of the site) shall be assessed by all parties to the venture.

> **注意** "加以"表示被动语态；逗号之间的连接用and；"由"表示被动语态。

第六条 合营企业设董事会，其人数组成由合营各方协商，在合同、章程中确定，并由合营各方委派和撤换。

Article 6 An equity joint venture shall have a board of directors; the number of the directors thereof from each party and composition of the board shall be stipulated in the contract and articles of association after consultation among the parties to the venture; such directors shall be appointed and replaced by the relevant parties.

> **注意** 专有名词"董事会"的翻译；"人数组成"表示"人数"和"组成"；"由"表示被动语态。

董事长和副董事长由合营各方协商确定或由董事会选举产生。

The chairman and the vice-chairman (vice-chairmen) shall be determined through consultation by the parties to the venture or elected by the board of directors.

 "副董事长"的翻译;"由"表示被动语态。

中外合营者的一方担任董事长的,由他方担任副董事长。
If the Chinese side or the foreign side assumes the office of the chairman, the other side shall assume the office(s) of vice-chairman (vice-chairmen).

 "担任"可以用assume翻译;专业名词"副董事长"的翻译。

董事会根据平等互利的原则,决定合营企业的重大问题。
The board of directors shall decide on important problems concerning the joint venture on the principle of equality and mutual benefit.

 中英文语序的差异,辅助语"根据平等互利的原则"应放在什么地方翻译。

董事会的职权是按合营企业章程规定,讨论决定合营企业的一切重大问题:
The functions and powers of the board of directors are, as stipulated in the articles of association of the equity joint venture, to discuss and decide all major issues concerning the venture, namely,

 "职权"可以理解为"职"和"权";冒号可以翻译为namely,表示"即是"。

企业发展规划、生产经营活动方案、收支预算、利润分配、劳动工资计划、停业，以及总经理、副总经理、总工程师、总会计师、审计师的任命或聘请及其职权和待遇等。

the venture's development plans, proposals for production and business operations, the budget for revenues and expenditure, the distribution of profits, the plans concerning manpower and wages, the termination of business, and the appointment or employment of the general manager, the vice-general manager(s), the chief engineer, the treasurer and the auditors, as well as the determination of their functions, powers and terms of employment, etc.

 本句中的专业名词较多，需要记忆；本句和上句有直接联系，需要联系翻译。

正副总经理（或正副厂长）由合营各方分别担任。

The offices of general manager and vice-general manager(s) (or factory manager and deputy manager(s)) shall be assumed by the respective parties to the venture.

 本句隐藏主语"的职位"；"由"表示被动语态。

合营企业职工的雇用、解雇，依法由合营各方的协议、合同规定。

The employment and discharge of the workers and staff members of an equity joint venture shall be stipulated in accordance with the law in the agreement and contract concluded by the parties to the venture.

 "职工"应当理解为"工人"和"职员"；"由"表示被动语态。

第七条　合营企业获得的毛利润，按《中华人民共和国税法》规定缴纳合营企业所得税后，扣除合营企业章程规定的储备基金、职工奖励及福利基金、企业发展基金，净利润根据合营各方注册资本的比例进行分配。

Article 7 The net profit of an equity joint venture shall be distributed among the parties to the joint venture in proportion to their respective contributions to the registered capital, after payment out of its gross profit of the equity joint venture income tax, pursuant to the provisions of the tax laws of the People's Republic of China, and after deductions from the gross profit of a reserve fund, a bonus and welfare fund for workers and staff members and a venture expansion fund, as stipulated in the venture's articles of association.

注意　本句较难；专业名词较多，如"毛利润"、"所得税"和"储备基金"等如何翻译；"净利润根据合营各方注册资本的比例进行分配"前都是辅助语，注意如何进行排序。

合营企业依照国家有关税收的法律和行政法规的规定，可以享受减税、免税的优惠待遇。

An equity joint venture may, in accordance with provisions of the relevant laws and administrative rules and regulations of the State on taxation, enjoy preferential treatment for tax reductions or exemptions.

注意　法律英语翻译一般不改变句子的语序，防止歧义出现。

外国合营者将分得的净利润用于在中国境内再投资时，可申请退还已缴纳的部分所得税。

A foreign joint venturer that reinvests its share of the net profit within Chinese territory may apply for a partial refund of the income tax already paid.

 逗号前的句子可以用主谓结构的偏正译法。

第八条　合营企业应凭营业执照在国家外汇管理机关允许经营外汇业务的银行或其他金融机构开立外汇账户。

Article 8 An equity joint venture shall, on the strength of its business license, open a foreign exchange account with a bank or and other financial institution which is permitted by the State agency for foreign exchange control to handle foreign exchange transactions.

 "应凭"如何翻译；"应凭营业执照在国家外汇管理机关允许经营外汇业务的银行或其他金融机构"都是辅助语，其位置处理得十分妥当。

合营企业的有关外汇事宜，应遵照《中华人民共和国外汇管理条例》办理。

An equity joint venture shall handle its foreign exchange transactions in accordance with the regulations on foreign exchange control of the People's Republic of China.

 汉译英换主语的问题，寻找隐藏主语在汉译英时十分重要。

合营企业在其经营活动中，可直接向外国银行筹措资金。

An equity joint venture may, in its business operations, directly raise funds from foreign banks.

法律英语汉译英时尽量保证原有语序，以免造成歧义。

合营企业的各项保险应向中国的保险公司投保。

The various kinds of insurance coverage of an equity joint venture shall be furnished by Chinese insurance companies.

 "投保"一词该如何翻译；而且注意寻找句子中隐藏的被动语态。

第九条 合营企业生产经营计划，应报主管部门备案，并通过经济合同方式执行。

Article 9 The production and business operating plans of an equity joint venture shall be submitted to the competent authorities for record and shall be implemented through economic contracts.

 "应报"表示被动语态；最后一个分句"并通过经济合同方式执行"也应该翻译为被动语态。

合营企业所需原材料、燃料、配套件等，应尽先在中国购买。

In its purchase of required raw and processed materials, fuels, auxiliary equipment, etc., an equity joint venture should first give priority to purchases in China.

 寻找汉译英的隐藏主语；并注意"应尽先在中国购买"可以翻译为should first give priority to purchases in China，属于典型的谓语动词过渡。

合营企业也可自筹外汇，直接在国际市场上购买。

It may also make such purchases directly on the world market with foreign exchange raised by itself.

 上句提到的名词可以用代词代替；并注意"购买"翻译为 make such purchases，属于典型的谓语动词过渡。

鼓励合营企业向中国境外销售产品。

An equity joint venture shall be encouraged to market its products outside China.

 无主语句应寻找真正的主语，也可翻译为被动语态。

出口产品可由合营企业直接或与其有关的委托机构向国外市场出售，也可通过中国的外贸机构出售。

It may sell its export products on foreign markets directly or through associated agencies or China's foreign trade agencies.

 寻找句子中间的隐藏主语；句中的一些专业名词，如"有关的委托机构"、"国外市场"和"中国的外贸机构"的翻译亦很重要。

合营企业产品也可在中国市场销售。

Its products may also be sold on the Chinese market.

 "可"表示被动语态的含义。

合营企业需要时可在中国境外设立分支机构。

Whenever necessary, an equity joint venture may set up branches and subbranches outside China.

> **注意** 在金融业中"分支机构"如何翻译。

第十条 外国合营者在履行法律和协议、合同规定的义务后分得的净利润，在合营企业期满或者中止时所分得的资金以及其他资金，可按合营企业合同规定的货币，按外汇管理条例汇往国外。

Article 10 The net profit which a foreign joint venturer receives as its share after performing its obligations under the laws, and the agreements or the contract, the funds it receives upon the expiration of the venture's term of operation or the suspension thereof, and its other funds may be remitted abroad in accordance with foreign exchange control regulations and in the currency or currencies specified in the contract concerning the equity joint venture.

> **注意** 本句的主语为"净利润"、"资金"和"其他资金"，这些主语前的定语较多，注意使用从句和分词结构；而且这些专业名词也要注意翻译准确。

鼓励外国合营者将可汇出的外汇存入中国银行。

A foreign joint venturer shall be encouraged to deposit in the Bank of China foreign exchange which is entitled to remit abroad.

> **注意** 无主语句应当寻找隐藏主语或使用被动语态；并且注意"中国银行"的翻译。

Speeches

Speech by President Nixon of the United States at Welcoming Banquet
美国总统尼克松在欢迎会上的讲话

本文选自于美国总统尼克松1972年访华时的一段讲话,由外交部翻译室翻译,属于典型的非文学翻译。演讲往往正式而生动,富有强烈的时代气息和感情色彩,翻译时句子结构复杂,语言要求正式上口,需要多考虑听众的感受,还特别需要注意时代背景。

Mr. Prime Minister and all of your distinguished guests this evening,
总理先生,今天晚上所有的诸位贵宾:

 领导人在寒暄时的说法。

On behalf of all of your American guests, I wish to thank you for the incomparable hospitality for which the Chinese people are justly famous throughout the world.

我谨代表你们的所有美国客人向你们表示感谢,感谢你们无可比拟的盛情款待。中国人民以这种盛情款待而闻名世界。

> **注意** on behalf of表示"谨代表";第二个分句的重译法需要注意;最后一个定语从句for which the Chinese people are justly famous throughout the world可以单独成句。

I particularly want to pay tribute, not only to those who prepared the magnificent dinner, but also to those who have provided the splendid music.

我们不仅要特别赞扬准备了这次盛大晚宴的人,而且还要赞扬为我们演奏美好音乐的人。

> **注意** 并列套用定语从句not only to those who...but also to those who的翻译方法。

Never have I heard American music played better in a foreign land.

我在外国从来没有听到过演奏得比这还要好的美国音乐。

> **注意** 否定词never位于句首引起句子的部分倒装,而且要注意从语法的角度而言,否定加比较级尽管表示最高级,但是翻译时不用最高级翻译,直接翻译为比较级加否定。

Mr. Prime Minister, I wish to thank you for your very gracious and eloquent remarks.

总理先生,我要感谢你的非常盛情和雄辩的讲话。

> **注意** wish to属于谓语动词的过渡;gracious and eloquent两个形容词翻译需要注意。

Unit 10　Speeches

At this very moment through the wonder of telecommunications, more people are seeing and hearing what we say than on any other such occasion in the whole history of the world.

此时此刻，通过电讯的奇迹，看到和听到我们讲话的人比在整个世界历史上任何其他这样的场合的人都要多。

 wonder这个词的翻译很重要；比较级more的翻译更有特点，第二个分句运用了主谓结构的偏正译法。

Yet, what we say here will not be long remembered.

不过，我们在这里所讲的话，人们不会长久地记住。

 要将what翻译出来，代词指明要点。

What we do here can change the world.

但我们在这里所做的事却能改变世界。

 和上一句合译，因为句子较短，而且注意需要有连词。

As you said in your toast, the Chinese people are a great people, the American people are a great people.

正如你在祝酒时讲的那样，中国人民是伟大的人民，美国人民是伟大的人民。

 后面两句之间的标点，没有连词，在翻译的时候也不能用连词"和"等，领导人讲话需要注意历史背景，表面上的语法错误可能蕴含着强烈的感情色彩。

If our two people are enemies the future of this world we share together is dark indeed.

我们两国人民要是互相为敌，那么我们共同居住的这个世界的前景就的确很暗淡了。

 英译汉时关联词双双出现；share这个单词翻译为"居住"。

But if we can find common ground to work together, the chance for world peace is immeasurably increased.

但是，我们如果能够找到进行合作的共同点，那么实现世界和平的机会就将大大增加。

 第二个分句中有抽象名词chance，没有动词词根，需要增词。

In the spirit of frankness which I hope will characterize our talks this week, let us recognize at the outset these points: we have times in the past been enemies.

我希望我们这个星期的会谈将是坦率的。本着这种坦率的精神，让我们在一开始就认识到这样几点：过去一些时候我们曾是敌人。

 I hope是插入语的译法；characterize需要进行意译；冒号之后的句子需要把时间状语整理清楚，分别翻译。

We have great differences today.

至今我们有巨大的分歧。

Unit 10　Speeches　193

> **注意** differences需要翻译为"分歧",而不是"差异"。

What brings us together is that we have common interests which transcend those differences.

让我们走到一起的原因,是我们有超越这些分歧的共同利益。

> **注意** 主语从句当中有what表示"原因";定语从句which transcend those differences较短,需要前置翻译。

As we discuss our differences, neither of us will compromise our principles.

在我们讨论分歧时,我们双方都不会在自己的原则上妥协。

> **注意** neither of us翻译为"双方……不",不翻译为"哪一个都不",英文重个体,中文重整体。

But while we cannot close the gulf between us, we can try to bridge it so that we may be able to talk across it.

但是,我们虽然不能弥合双方之间的鸿沟,我们却能够设法搭一座桥,以便我们能够越过它进行会谈。

> **注意** gulf如何翻译;bridge需要翻译为动词;talk across不是动词词组,需要分开翻译。

Speech by Former U.S. President Carter at Welcoming Banquet
美国前总统卡特在欢迎宴会上的讲话

本文选自于美国总统卡特1986年访华时的一段讲话,由外交部翻译室翻译,属于典型的非文学翻译。其内容多样,涉及政治、经济、文化等各个方面,所以在选择做翻译练习时,可以多选领导人讲话为材料。

Permit me first to thank our Chinese hosts for your extraordinary arrangements and hospitality.

首先,请允许我对中国的主办方表示感谢,感谢你们十分出色的安排和款待。

first为插入语,需要提到句首翻译;句子中间应该有重译法。

My wife and I, as well as our entire party, are deeply grateful.
我的夫人和我以及全体随行人员都深为感激。

前面的主语直接翻译,不需要翻译为"我和我的夫人",非文学翻译忠实于原文;party翻译为"随行人员"。

In the short period of six days, we have gone a longer distance than the Long March.
在过去短短六天里,我们所走的路程比长征的路程还长。

longer需要在句末翻译;后一个分句主谓结构的偏正译法。

We have acquired a keen sense of the diversity, dynamism, and progress of China under your policies of reform and opening to the outside world.

我们强烈地感受到你们执行的改革和对外开放政策给中国带来的多样化、活力和进步。

> **注意** acquired a keen sense of是典型的谓语动词过渡；diversity, dynamism, and progress是典型的抽象名词，无动词词根，所以增动词"带来"。

More than eight years have passed since Vice Premier Deng Xiaoping and I joined hands to establish full diplomatic relations between our two great nations.

自从邓小平副总理和我共同建立我们两个伟大国家之间的正式外交关系以来，已经八年多了。

> **注意** 时间状语从句可以置于句末翻译；diplomatic relations翻译为"外交关系"。

Our hope and vision was to forge a Sino-American relationship which would contribute to world peace and the welfare of our two peoples.

建立一种有利于世界和平和我们两国人民福祉的中美关系是我们当时的希望和憧憬。

> **注意** 主语较短时可以考虑放在句末翻译；定语从句which would contribute to world peace and the welfare of our two peoples的翻译很灵活。

I personally looked upon the forging of firm Sino-American ties as a historically significant experiment.

我本人把建立牢固的中美关系看做是具有历史意义的尝试。

> **注意** forging属于典型的抽象名词，有动词词根时，翻译为动词"建立"。

We faced the question in 1978, as to some extent we still do today:

在某种程度上，我们在1978年乃至今天面临的问题仍然是：

> **注意** as to some extent插入语表示观点，可以放在句首翻译；句首We faced the question in 1978采用主谓结构的偏正译法。

Can two nations as different as ours——yours one of the oldest civilizations on earth, mine one of the youngest;

我们两国迥然不同，贵国是地球上最古老的文明之一，我国是最年轻的国家之一；

> **注意** 问句较长时，可以将前面所有句子都翻译为肯定句，将最后一句翻译为问句；后两个分句没有连词，翻译时遵守原文的意思，不需要增加连词。

yours a socialist state and mine committed to capitalism; yours a developing country and mine a developed one——

贵国是社会主义国家，而我国致力于资本主义；贵国是发展中国家，而我国是发达国家；

> **注意** yours可以翻译为"贵国"，表示尊敬。

Unit 10　Speeches　197

can two nations surmount and indeed draw upon these differences to build an unprecedented and distinctive relationship in world affairs?

像这样的两个国家是否能够超越并利用这些差异，在世界事务中建立一种前所未有的、独具特色的关系？

本句无难点，注意单词的翻译即可。

If we are successful, in one great step our two nations will have been able to ease one of the greatest sources of tension in international affairs: that between the developing and developed worlds.

我们如果取得成功，我们两国就能迈出一大步，缓和国际事务中造成紧张的最大因素之一，即发展中世界与发达世界的关系。

英译汉时先说主语；sources属于抽象名词，没有动词词根，需要增词。

We still have a long way to go, and it is still too early to conclude that our experiment will culminate in success, but certainly the results of the first ten years are promising.

我们面前还有很长的路，现在断言我们的尝试将会圆满成功还为时过早，但是头十年所取得的成果肯定是富有成效的。

注意 too...to...结构不翻译为"太……而不能……"；results属于典型的抽象名词，无动词词根，可以增词"取得"。

Sino-American ties have become extensive, affecting all aspects of our national lives: commerce, culture, education, scientific exchange, and our separate national security policies.

中美关系现在变得非常广泛，涉及我们人民生活的各个方面：商业、文化、教育、科学交流，以及我们各自的国家安全政策。

英文中的逗号要翻译为中文的顿号。

增进相互了解 加强友好合作
——江泽民主席在美国哈佛大学的演讲

Enhance Mutual Understanding and Build Stronger Ties of Friendlyship and Cooperation
——Address by President Jiang Zemin at Harvard University of the United States of America

本文选自于1997年江泽民同志访问美国哈佛大学的一段讲话，由外交部翻译室翻译，属于典型的非文学翻译。文中中国特色词汇较多，表达十分灵活，中文句式以短句见长，翻译时注意前后句与句之间的联系。若有可能将文中的重要词汇熟记，对于各种翻译考试都有很大的益处。

校长先生，
Mr. President,
女士们，先生们：
Ladies and Gentlemen,

本句无难点，属于寒暄用语，直接翻译。

我感谢陆登庭校长的邀请，使我有机会在这美好的金秋时节，来到你们这座美国古老而又现代化的学府。

Unit 10 Speeches   199

I wish to thank President Rudenstine for inviting me to this old yet modern institution of the United States in this golden fall.

 wish to是对强势动词thank的过渡；"金秋"翻译为golden fall；"而"翻译为yet，表示承接关系。

哈佛建校三百六十年来，培养出许多杰出的政治家、科学家、文学家和企业家，曾出过六位美国总统，三十多位诺贝尔奖获得者。

Since its founding some 360 years ago, Harvard has nurtured a great number of outstanding statesmen, scientists, writers and businessmen, including six of the American Presidents and over thirty Nobel Prize winners.

 中英文主从句与代词的关系，中文第一个句子用名词，第二个句子用名词或是代词，但是英文是主句用名词，从句用代词；"培养"翻译为nurture；专有名词要会翻译。

先有哈佛，后有美利坚合众国，这说明了哈佛在美国历史上的地位。

The fact that Harvard was founded before the United States of America testifies to its position in the American history.

 将"这"翻译the fact that...，可以形成典型的同位语从句结构。

哈佛是最早接受中国留学生的美国大学之一。

Harvard is among the first America universities to accept Chinese students.

 本句中的定语"最早接受中国留学生的"翻译为不定式，也可以用定语从句。

中国教育界、科学界、文化界一直同哈佛大学保持着学术交流。

The Chinese educational, scientific and cultural communities have all along maintained academic exchanges with this university.

 "界"的翻译，其余专业名词要会翻译。

哈佛为增进中美两国人民的相互了解作出了有益的贡献。

Harvard has thus made useful contribution to the enhanced mutual understanding between the Chinese and American peoples.

 thus一词没有任何含义，只是语气词；专业名词"相互了解"的翻译很经典。

相互了解，是发展国与国之间关系的前提。

Mutual understanding is the basis for state-to-state relations.

 句中出现"发展"，翻译成英语后可以省略。

唯有相互了解，才能增进信任，加强合作。

Without it, it would be impossible for countries to build trust and promote cooperation with one another.

第一个分句和上句有直接关系，翻译成虚拟语气由without 引导。

中美建交以来，我们两国人民之间的相互交流与了解在逐渐扩大和加深。

Since the establishment of diplomatic ties between China and the United States, the exchanges and mutual understanding between our two peoples have broadened and deepened steadily.

 第一个分句主谓结构翻译为偏正结构；后面句子中专业名词"相互交流与了解"注意翻译。

但还不够。

However, this is not enough.

 本句无难点，直接翻译。

为了推动中美关系的发展，中国需要进一步了解美国，美国也需要进一步了解中国。

To promote the development of China-U.S. relations, China need to know the United States better and vice versa.

 本句后面两个分句不能直接翻译，要用vice versa的译法。

中国在自己发展的长河中，形成了优良的历史文化传统，这些传统，随着时代变迁和社会进步获得扬弃和发展。

In the prolonged course of its development, China has formed its fine historical and cultural traditions, which have been either developed or sublated with the changes of the times and social progress.

 中文先说主语再说辅助语，英文相反；第二个逗号后面的"传统"一词和前一句的"传统"重合，可以用定语从句翻译；"扬弃"属于哲学词汇，在这里用德语词汇翻译。

这些传统对今天中国人的价值观念、生活方式和中国的发展道路，具有深刻的影响。

These traditions have exerted a profound impact on the values and way of life of the Chinese people today, and on China's road of advance.

 "对……产生影响"该如何翻译；"发展道路"该如何翻译。

这里，我想就以下一些方面谈些看法，希望有助于诸位对中国的了解。

Here, I would like to make some observations on the following aspects which I hope will help you know China better.

 "想法"该如何翻译；第二个逗号后的句子可以翻译为定语从句，实际上也可以翻译为并列结构。

一是团结统一的传统。

First, the tradition of solidarity and unity.

 "团结统一"该如何翻译。

中华民族是由五十六个民族组成的大家庭。

The Chinese nation is a big family composed of fifty-six nationalities.

 中文里定语从句"五十六个民族组成的"前置，英文中可以翻译为过去分词做定语。

从遥远的古代起，我国各族人民就建立了紧密的政治经济文化联系，共同开发了祖国的河山。

Since time immemorial, people of all our nationalities have established close-knit political, economic and cultural links and joined hands in developing the vast land of our country.

 本句无难点，需要注意专业名词"遥远的古代"和"政治经济文化联系"的译法。

两千多年前就形成了幅员广阔的统一国家。

China became a vast unified country more than two thousand years ago.

 "幅员辽阔"该如何翻译。

悠久的中华文化，成为维系民族团结和国家统一的牢固纽带。

The age-old Chinese culture becomes a strong bond for ethnic harmony and national unity.

 "民族团结"和"国家统一"该如何翻译。

团结统一，深深印在中国人的民族意识中。

Solidarity and unity are deeply inscribed in the hearts of the Chinese people as part of their national identity.

谓语"印在"该如何翻译,"民族意识"该如何翻译。

中国历史上虽曾出现过暂时的分裂现象,但民族团结和国家统一始终是中华民族历史的主流,是中国发展进步的重要保障。

Despite occasional divisions, ethnic harmony and national unity have remained the main stream in the history of the Chinese nation, and an important guarantee for China's development and progress.

"中国历史上"为状语,可以放在句末翻译;"出现过"为弱势动词,可以省略;这句话最重要的就是如何处理让步状语"虽曾出现过暂时的分裂现象"的结构,请仔细理解。

新中国的成立,标志着中华民族实现了空前的大团结。

The founding of the People's Republic of China in 1949 marked an unprecedented great unity of the Chinese nation.

谓语动词"标志"的译法以及形容词"空前的"的译法。

各民族之间建立了平等、团结、互助的新型关系。

A new type of relationship of equality, solidarity and mutual assistance among all our nationalities has been established.

注意 汉语里隐藏被动语态的存在,英文善于使用被动语态。

各民族人民依法享有各项权利和自由。

Unit 10　Speeches

People of all our nationalities enjoy full rights and freedoms provided for by the law.

 "依法"该如何翻译。

在少数民族聚居的地方实行了区域自治。
In places where there is a high concentration of ethnic minorities, regional autonomy is in practice.

 汉译英有时也需要断句，"在……地方"可以翻译为定语从句；"区域自治"该如何翻译。

民族地区的经济社会获得不断的发展。
These regions have witnessed continued economic and social development.

 "获得"为本句谓语，且注意用何种词汇翻译。

所有这些，为巩固国家统一奠定了坚实的政治基础。
All these have laid a solid political foundation for consolidated national unity.

 "奠定基础"该如何翻译。

二是独立自主的传统。
Second, the tradition of maintaining independence.

 "独立自主"该如何翻译。

我们的先人历来把独立自主视为立国之本。

Our ancestors always regarded the spirit of maintaining independence as the foundation of a nation.

 "立国之本"该如何翻译。

中国作为人类文明发祥地之一,在几千年的历史进程中,文化传统始终没有中断。

As one of the cradles of human civilization, China has all along maintained its cultural tradition without letup in its history of several thousand years.

 主语、辅助语和主要内容之间的关系和排序;两个状语"作为人类文明发祥地之一,在几千年的历史进程中"位于句首,需要前后分配翻译。

近代中国虽屡遭列强欺凌,国势衰败。

In modern times, the frequent bullying and humiliation by imperialist powers once weakened China.

 逗号前后之间的关系;"列强"的翻译。

但经过全民族的百年抗争,又以巨人的姿态重新站立起来。

However, after a hundred years' struggle of the entire Chinese nation, China has stood up again as a giant.

 "姿态"为范畴词,可以不译,直接省略;第二个分句需要增主语。

这充分说明，中国人独立自主的民族精神具有坚不可摧的力量。

This fully testifies to the indestructible strength of this independent national spirit of the Chinese people.

 "具有"为"力量"在表示的抽象名词时所增的词，所以在翻译时需要省略，"说明"后面的分句可以译成短语。

今天，我们在探索自己的发展道路时，坚持从中国国情出发，来解决如何进行经济政治文化建设的问题，而不照搬别国的模式。

Today, in finding a road of advance suited to us, we will proceed from our own national conditions to address the problems of how to attain economic, political and cultural development without blindly copying other countries' models.

 各分句之间的连接；句与句之间需要什么样的连词很重要，可以用连词，不定式或是分词。

在处理国际事务中，我们采取独立自主的立场和政策。

In handling international affairs, we decide our positions and policies from an independent approach.

 专业名词"国际事务"和"独立自主"该如何翻译。

中国人民珍惜同各国人民的友谊与合作，也珍惜自己经过长期奋斗而得来的独立自主权利。

The Chinese people cherish its friendship and cooperation with other peoples, and they also cherish their right to independence, which they have won through protracted struggles.

 第二个分句中的定语从句"自己经过长期奋斗而得来的"的翻译。

三是爱好和平的传统。
Third, the peace-loving tradition.

 本句无难点，直接翻译。

我国先秦思想家就提出了"亲仁善邻，国之宝也"的思想。
Chinese thinkers of the pre-Qin days (over 2,000 years ago) advanced the doctrine "loving people and treating neighbors kindly are most valuable to a country".

 本句需要增词解释"先秦"；两句古文如何翻译。

这反映了自古以来中国人民就希望天下太平、同各国人民友好相处。
This is a reflection of the aspiration of the Chinese people for a peaceful world where people of all countries live in harmony.

 谓语动词"反映"翻译为名词is a reflection of，这是典型的抽象名词的译语；"反映"和"希望"该如何翻译。

今天，专心致志进行现代化建设的中国人民，更需有一个长期和平的国际环境和良好的周边环境。
Today, the Chinese people who are committed to modernization

need more than ever a long-term international environment of peace and a favorable neighboring environment.

 定语从句"专心致志进行现代化建设的"该如何翻译；专业名词"长期和平的国际环境"和"良好的周边环境"该如何翻译。

我国的对外政策，是以和平为宗旨的。
China's foreign policy is peace-oriented.

 "中国的外交政策"该如何翻译；China's 和 Chinese的区别。

我们坚持在和平共处五项原则，特别是在相互尊重、平等互利、互不干涉内政的原则基础上，同世界各国建立和发展友好合作关系。

We will establish and develop friendly relations and cooperation with all countries in the world on the basis of the Five Principles of Peaceful Coexistence, especially the principles of mutual respect, equality and mutual benefit and non-interference in each other's internal affairs.

 中文主句和辅助语的关系，"我们"为主语，"建立和发展"为谓语，中间全是辅助语，在翻译时需要改变位置；"和平共处五项原则"该如何翻译；"相互尊重、平等互利、互不干涉内政"该如何翻译。

我们绝不会把自己曾经遭受欺凌的苦难加之于人。
We will never impose upon others the kind of sufferings we ourselves once experienced.

定语从句"自己曾经遭受欺凌的"的翻译。

中国的发展与进步,不会对任何人构成威胁。
A developing and progressing China does not pose a threat to anyone.

 偏正短语"中国的发展与进步"的主谓译法。

将来中国富强起来了,也永远不称霸。
China will never seek hegemony even if it grows rich and strong in the future.

 "称霸"该如何翻译;主句和从句之间运用了条件关系来翻译。

中国始终是维护世界和平与地区稳定的坚定力量。
China is always a staunch force for world peace and regional stability.

 "坚定"该如何翻译。

四是自强不息的传统。
Fourth, the tradition of constantly striving to strengthen oneself.

 "自强不息"该如何翻译。

我们的先哲通过观察宇宙万物的变动不居,提出了"天行健,君子以自强不息"的思想。

Through observing the changing nature of the universe and of all things, ancient Chinese philosophers proposed the following doctrine: "Heaven operates vigorously, and gentlemen exert to strengthen themselves unceasingly."

> 注意 主语"我们的先哲"与辅助语"通过观察宇宙万物的变动不居"之间的关系；古文"天行健，君子以自强不息"的翻译。

这成为激励中国人民变革创新、努力奋斗的精神力量。

This idea has become an important moral force spurring the Chinese people to work hard for change and innovation.

> 注意 定语"变革创新、努力奋斗的"的翻译。

中国古代文明的发展，是中华民族艰苦奋斗、自强不息的结果。

The fruits of China's ancient civilization were brought about by the tireless efforts and hard work of the Chinese nation.

> 注意 句式的变化，不再是"发展是结果"的译法，而是运用了被动语态的译法；其中四字短语"艰苦奋斗"和"自强不息"的译法很重要。

近百年来，为了摆脱半殖民地半封建的历史境遇，中国人民进行了艰苦卓绝、奋发图强的斗争。

In the past one hundred years or so, the Chinese people waged arduous struggles to lift themselves from their historical plight under semi-colonial and semi-feudal rule.

> **注意** 双状语"近百年来,为了摆脱半殖民地半封建的历史境遇"出现在句首时,需要前后分配翻译;四字短语"艰苦卓绝、奋发图强"的译法;"历史境遇"后需要增词。

中国民主革命的先行者孙中山首先提出"振兴中华"的口号。

Dr. Sun Yat-sen, China's fore-runner in the democratic revolution, was the first to put forward the slogan of "rejuvenation of China".

> **注意** "孙中山"的翻译方法;"中国民主革命的先行者"与"孙中山"是同位语,注意翻译方法;四字短语"振兴中华"的翻译亦很重要。

他领导的辛亥革命,推翻了在中国延续几千年的君主专制制度。

He led the Revolution of 1911 to overthrow the autocratic monarchy lasting several millennia in China.

> **注意** 第一个分句,偏正短语的主谓译法;后面的句子需要用连词和第一个分句连接,用to连接表示目的。

在毛泽东思想指引下,中国共产党领导中国人民实现了民族独立和人民解放,并把中国建设成为初步繁荣昌盛的社会主义国家。

Under the guidance of Mao Zedong Thought, the Communist Party of China led the Chinese people in achieving China's national independence and people's liberation and in building China into a socialist country with initial prosperity.

Unit 10　Speeches

 专业名词"毛泽东思想"、"中国共产党"、"民族独立"和"人民解放"等的译法；动词之间的关系处理得很恰当。

今天，在邓小平理论指引下，我国人民坚定不移地实行改革开放，在现代化建设中取得了举世瞩目的成就。

Today, guided by Deng Xiaoping Theory, the Chinese people are firmly pressing ahead with reform and opening-up and have achieved remarkable successes in the modernization drive.

 专业名词"邓小平理论"、"改革开放"和"现代化建设"的译法；"坚定不移"该如何翻译；"举世瞩目"该如何翻译。

中国进入了百年来发展最快最好的历史时期。

China has entered a period of its fastest and healthiest growth in this century.

注意 "历史时期"的翻译方法。